she's got a ticket...

By Juliet Awang

Acknowledgements

I would like to give my deepest thanks to my wonderful friend Paula, I couldn't have finished this without her guidance in turning my grammatically error laden manuscript into a legible book.

I would also like to give my deepest thanks to another wonderful friend, Sarah! Your kind assistance in all matters of printing has helped me turn my written pages into a fully-fledged book.

Foreword

This story is based on the true events of life. Not all things are written in true form...my story is an embellished tale. The parts that are embellished will remain with me, and have been embellished for my family's protection.

The points within the story that are important are the truth.

I dedicate this book to my three beautiful son's. The three of you are everything to me, and my love for you all is infinite. I couldn't have ever even dreamed my life would be so full of love until I found you three.

And lastly to John, for without your input none of this would have happened...the good or the bad. The darkness or the light.

"Sooner or later all the people of the world will have to find a way to live together in peace" Martin Luther King Jnr

Chapter One

I breezed into the VIP area of Manchester Airport with Jack, his friend Chunk, and his girlfriend Lippy. We made our way towards the luxury leather seats overlooking the huge windows and settled in to watch the planes taxiing and taking off to and from their destinations, whilst we all sipped Dom Perignon Champagne, waiting for our scheduled flight to New York City. I can't deny I was excited, happy even. Things had been relatively good between Jack and me for some time now...so yeah, I was excited.

We boarded our plane - club class - and headed off over the Atlantic Ocean, all of us merry with excitement...and a little Champagne.
On our arrival at JFK airport, we jumped straight into a yellow cab, we were planning on getting a Limo - standard over there I had been told - but I really wanted the experience of that yellow New York cab.
We arrived at the hotel and it was fantastic, it had an art-deco vibe to it. It was all marble floors, and tiled walls of black, cream and gold diamond shapes. It buzzed with excitement from the array of visitors mingling around in the reception. It was situated around the corner from New York's Broadway. We checked-in with an overzealous receptionist, who gave us our room keys. "You are on the fourth floor up Sir, and to your left. The elevator is just around the corner here. We are here if you need anything. Have a nice day, and I hope you enjoy your stay with us here at the Americano. The concierge will bring up your luggage shortly" he informed us.

We put our flight bags into our rooms and headed out. The first place I wanted to see was 5th Avenue. I walked out into the lobby and through the huge glass doors into the streets of New York. As the icy cold air hit, it stung my face, I pulled my scarf up and my hat down over my ears. You could still see the remains of snowfall from a few days before glistening out from the corners. As soon I stepped outside I was entranced by the buildings...wow! My eyes continually wandering upwards, you could barely see the sky the buildings are that high. I now understand the meaning of skyscraper. There was an instant buzz about the place, all the shops, the lights, the people - of all walks of life, going about in their own world, uninterested in mine or anyone else's for that matter. The New Yorkers all move about with vigour, determination and speed, no time to stop, no time to see. They all had places to go and things to do.

Time Square!!! Time Square!! It was the first place Jack and I came to, not a great distance from our hotel. I had seen this many times on television, this iconic image, and there I was standing in it. Surrounding the triangle are a multitude of shops, there's a big double golden arch - McDonald's, everywhere you go there's a McDonald's. Bank of America, with its orange background and blue writing, all lit up in its huge sign. There were bars and diners scattered about amongst the other shops that make up the triangle of Time Square. Bright advertisements are everywhere, for The Phantom of the Opera and many other Broadway shows. The biggest HMV I've ever seen, advertising - James Gandolfini & co from Soprano's coming in to sign copies of their DVD. There is one huge screen after another, on top of each other, next to each other. It was a huge advertising plot. The lights flash about like a rainbow in the air, the vibe buzzing from one thing to the next. I was mesmerized. It was like I'd just stepped into the television. The place felt electrifying. The colours from all the advertising screens had me looking from one brightly lit screen to the next, trying but failing to take it all in.

Walking up 5th Avenue, I am overwhelmed by the vastness of the buildings, the enormity of the streets; the sidewalks are as big as the roads at home. I can see why they say the streets are paved in gold; the wealth is evident in every corner. Where there is wealth you will always see there is poverty, and it must be the worst place on earth to be so down on your luck, having to witness those who lavish in being so up on theirs whilst you are trying to survive. There are more screens, advertising beautiful perfumes and bags and clothes. Some of the architecture had a distinct gothic feel, all pointy wooden window frames and crafted stone spires, some definitely art deco with their ornate shaping. Built in the days after WW1, at a time when the world began to put technological advances firmly on the map, and merged technology with craftsmanship. Others were like uninspiring Lego buildings made of brown brick. All of them where so high, you get a crooked neck walking round New York City. In this part of 5th Avenue the ground floor of all the buildings had expensive shops leasing space from whoever owned them. All adorned with their own take on uniqueness, an extravagant Christmas display in every shop window, entrancing the passes by to stop and look. The yellow cabs flying past you, the hot dog vendors on every corner, the sound of Santa Claus' ringing their bells and the scent of roasted chestnuts drifted in from all sides. The constant roar of traffic, the noise of mass people scuttling about is a constant companion. Jack and I came to the Versace

store, just beyond the entrance stood a gigantic solid gold lion. It was absolutely enormous, it stood in the middle of a rounded marble and glass staircase, and it was as high as two floors. I stood at the window and observed all the different customers buzzing around. One particular guy sat on the plush, luxurious purple couch - with his big hairy brown dog by his feet. The assistants looked even more glamorous than the customers. They all seemed to be lavishing attention on this one customer. One lady, a very pretty blonde, with just enough make-up to accentuate her features, wearing a beautifully sophisticated black Versace dress brought out an array of different items.
"Three of them, different colours", he said wagging his finger.
"Two of those!" he demanded.

'This must be how the truly rich live Jennifer' I thought to myself. That's me Jennifer Smith...twenty-four-year-old woman from Liverpool...about to go into the Versace store in New York City. The kind of place I'd never dreamt I would get to visit, but life had taken me down a path that now brought such luxuries into my life...this I would come to learn was at a price...but not yet. We walked in to join the customers and do some shopping of our own.

We dined in Little Italy one night. The tables where lined with chequered table cloths and on the floor a scattering of saw dust, for an authentic feel of a genuine Old Italian Restaurant. Chunk and Jack each cracking some 'wise guy' joke. "I'm gonna make you an offer you cannot refuse..."
"Say hello to my little friend..."
The next night we ate in China Town.
We visited the Empire State building, where you can see the enormity of the streets of New York City. 1st Avenue - 11th Avenue, 1st street - 145th street all crisscrossed into an interlocking grid. We toured the Statue of Liberty by helicopter at night, another amazing experience.
One evening Jack and I even caught a showing of The Phantom of 'The Opera' on Broadway.
We skated around the Ice-rink in Central Park, well I did. Jack couldn't. It made me laugh to watch him, I'd be whizzing around, skating with all the New Yorkers, fast and fearless. He was there on the edge every time I'd pass him. Trying to skate, but failing, two left feet splayed out, he looked like Bambi. It was hilarious. The ice-rink was huge, just like everything else in New York. It had begun to snow again that morning, and I knew if I took

a picture it would look just like a Christmas card. It was as magical as it looks.

We visited St. Patrick's Cathedral, the most amazing church I had ever visited. It sits elegantly alone among the other buildings that surround it. There are huge oak doors within the three colossal arched spires at the front, that are polished to perfection; the yellow sandstone walls making the doors stand out magnificently. I smelt the familiar smell of incense that comes from a church as I entered through the statuesque open doors. We were both in awe looking at the mammoth pillars that stand majestically throughout, gazing at the multitude of stained glass windows painting a story of biblical scriptures. As we walked through the aisle, past a row of wooden pews, we turned to the side of the church. Towards a table full with lit candles flickering and dancing to the theme of somebody's wishes. We both put our dollar in the box and lit a candle. I got down on my knees and prayed, for another baby. Something we had both wanted; a new baby brother or sister for our son. I felt a deep sense that God was listening; knowing I wanted another baby to bless my life.

As our New York adventure was coming to a close we had special plans to dine at the top floor of The World Trade Centre. I stood in my hotel room looking in the mirror, admiring my fabulous new black lace Gucci dress. It was simply cut and clung in all the right places resting just above my knees. I pinned my hair at both sides and wondered whether to wear my new perfume Gucci by Gucci or my old Chanel number 5. I decided to go all out Gucci, my new perfume smelt of flowers and fruit with just a hint of something woody. I sprayed it in the air and as the mist descended I sauntered beneath it. I slipped on my shoes and wrapped my cashmere pashmina around my bare shoulders. We had ordered a limousine to take us there; it was waiting outside our hotel when we came down.

As we pulled up outside the Twin Towers I couldn't believe the size of the buildings. If I thought everything else was huge in New York then this was gargantuan, you couldn't even see the top. The towers themselves were rather nondescript and grey. However, entering the building was a different story. I could feel its magnitude; see its grandeur and splendour. Everything appeared to be made of marble, my mouth was agape the entire journey in. Getting the lift to the top floor was an experience all of its own. It felt like Charlie must have felt in that glass elevator. 107 floors up, oh my God!! It seemed to take forever.

As the elevator arrived and the mirrored doors slid open we were instantly greeted with a wondrous scene. We only had to take a few steps across the corridor and we were straight in the restaurant. The aroma drifting towards us was sublime, all herbs and spices, succulent meats and fishes, sweet desserts of strawberries, raspberries and white chocolate. The scent of garlic and seafood fluttered passed as a waiter walked by ready to serve another guest. The maître d' caught our eye as we walked towards him, "Hello and welcome to The Windows on the World Restaurant, do you have a reservation?" he ever so politely asked us. "Yeah Jack Jones, table for four!" Jack replied.

I wasn't paying too much attention I was observing the scene in front of me. All the tables were candle lit, and the entire room had strategically placed lighting, just enough for the waiters to see but not enough to spoil the ambience. They had tables in the centre of the room, and booths scattered around the edge. Varied in size, but all elegantly dressed with porcelain and silver. To my left sat an older couple holding hands across the table. They had finished what looked to be their main course. They looked in their forties, perhaps her a little older than him. Her shiny red hair was pinned up in a French twist, and the silver clip she wore in her hair sparkling as the light from the candles would catch it. She looked sophisticated and mature; I could see lust in both their eyes. He had a more serious look about him; he wore a tailored grey suit, no tie. The top buttons of his black shirt were undone. He caressed her hand as she softly chatted away to him.

In front of me sat a table of eight men, five of them of Asian origin, three of them American. I only realised this when they stopped speaking Mandarin and talked between themselves about ordering more wine. They all appeared happy and relaxed. As I watched them I imagined the deal they had just closed, a multi-million-dollar deal for the newest technological device. The waiter brought over their desserts, all delicate little parcels on over-sized plates.
"Jen, Jen! Are you coming?" Jack's voice pulling me back from my trance, so I followed him as he followed our friendly waiter over to a corner booth. Soon enough our conversation, laughter and the clinking of our glasses mixed in with the rest. Jack leant in towards me and whispered in my ear, "Who'd have thought it eh, two scruffs from Liverpool eating at top of The World Trade Centre!!"...that was us, two scruffs from Liverpool.

Our meal was 5 courses, my Hor d' oeuvres of snapper crudo with chillies and sesame, served in a shell was define. I had lobster bisque, then an arugula salad which is roasted pears, red onion and goat's cheese, followed by sweet-tart duck breast with cherry sauce, and to finish vanilla bean creme-brulee. It took some effort, but I managed. The wine and the champagne were flowing all night. By the time we left each of us were rather drunk, but I knew then that this was an experience I would remember forever.

On our final day Jack and I spent it mulling around New York City. We visited the bar of the famous Waldorf Astoria - wanting to meet Prince Zumunda!! The pair of us drank too much wine, and stumbled out of there rather giddy. We both giggled the entire way back to our hotel. "Hot-dawg, hot-dawg, anybody wanna hot-dawg!" Mucking around, something we had not done in far too long, something we once did a lot of. As we walked along laughing Jack's arm draped around my shoulder he pulled me in closer and told me he loved me as his lips planted a big kiss on my cheek. My heart swelled and I smiled as I looked at Jack and wondered where had this boy been, the one I fell in love with. I had missed him and was ecstatic to have him here with me having fun like the old days; the entire trip had done wonders for our relationship. It made me fall in love with him again. What can I say...I was a fool in his arms! Just before we rounded the corner to our hotel I stopped for a deli Sandwich - I just loved the way they talked "cawfee - tammatoe's on your sandwich?"

As we walked towards our room we bumped into Chunk, him and Lippy had been doing their own thing. Jack stopped for a chat, when he came back to the room he asked me if I minded if they went for a drink. "No not at all, I just want to have a bath, and pack. So feel free" I told him. Every day had been fantastic, but I was ready to go home and was pleased with the peace. So I sat and ate my sandwich, had a bath, and enjoyed the silence whilst I packed our bags.
I was lying on the bed half asleep when Jack came back, as soon as I caught eye contact with him I knew, that look in his eye. That look of rage, a look that signalled to me, once again he had succumbed to his vice. A blazing look, a look that changed from light to dark in the blink of an eye. My heart pounded in my chest, and in that moment my first feeling was not fear, it was shame. Ashamed that I had been stupid enough to belief it would never happen again.
He started rummaging rampantly through our things for something. "What's the matter?" I asked.

He shouted back, "I'm going back out, now where's my fucking money?"
"I think you've had enough Jack", I stated.
That was it. He flipped, screaming at me.
"You Slag!!! Where's my fucking money? Fucking Cunt!! I fucking hate you, you ugly boot!! Should of fucked them ho's instead of coming back to you!!"
Sadly, I'd heard this all before...seen him in this state before, cocaine churning through his body, turning him into the man that I hated and feared.
I tried my best to ignore him, but he wouldn't let up and confined to a hotel room, there was nowhere for me to go. He kept shouting all kinds of abuse at me, calling me all the names that had once hurt so much, but had now become something I was used to.
"I'm off to find someone to shag, you fucking slag!" His final insult before I retaliated.
"Fucking go you bastard! I'm sick of this shit. You swore you'd never touch that shit again, and fucking look at you!!!"
Well that was it, Jack flew at me. He dragged me by the hair off the bed. He swung his leg hard against my back. Me being me I couldn't help but fight back, when I'm pushed into a corner - in a fight or flight situation, I fight. I hit him back. He went berserk. Minutes of rage followed that have become a blur. I just knew I was scared and he was hurting me. The next thing I knew he threw me out into the corridor, where Chunk and Lippy were standing, as was security. Everyone could see the blazing look in his eyes. Chunk tried to intervene, "Fucking stay out of it you fat fucking cunt!!" he spluttered at Chunk.
Jack stormed into the room, slamming the door, rambling some incoherent babble to himself. The security tried to help, but I just ran into Chunk and Lippy's room, too embarrassed, ashamed and upset to look at any of them. Lippy took me into the bathroom. I could feel the blood trickling down my mouth. My back felt on fire, I knew I was hurt. As I pulled up my top I could see the red stinging bruises already appearing on my body, and shockingly - I had several bite marks on me. I heard this meek miniscule voice say these words "I never felt him do that"
...I crumbled to the floor and cried.

So this is it, this is what I'm trying to do here...tell you my story. The good, the bad and the ugly! That part I've just told you about was once something I never mentioned. Not that I was scared. I was ashamed. From the event itself, but also the fact it wasn't the first time he had hurt me.

After this he may never have hit me again, but he certainly hurt me. What I want to tell you about is how I got to a place where I feel no pain from that event or from Jack, or any pain from anyone else for that matter. Not anymore. A place where my heart forgave the human errors other people had inflicted on my soul, but more importantly...my own errors!
So I'll get on with the story...the flight home was early the next day, and as I sat in that airport withdrawn and tired, all I could think of was my son - Francis.

When I stood in the bathroom the next morning, looking at my body in the mirror I had wanted to crawl into a ball and hide. Why did he do this? Everything had been going so well. Yesterday I had been in love with him again. I felt our relationship move away from the destructive pattern we had come to live, and then he does this. Francis however was awaiting our return home, and home with him was where I needed to be. So I pulled my jumper over my battered body and wiped away my tears.
Returning home and hugging Francis was the only thing that helped, the pain in cuddling him hurt, but the contact from someone who loved me was desperately needed. Even though he had no idea what had happened. No one did, because I never told anyone.

How much did I love this man? Was love making me weak, foolish and incapable of standing on my own two feet??? All the things that I never thought I was. In fact, I viewed myself at the very infinite end of the spectrum on that. Yet here I was, hurt by this man, again! My heart, my soul, my mind had had enough. I knew on every level it was over between us. This would be the last time he would hurt my heart...

Despite all that had happened, it was Christmas, and Francis always came first for me. Jack would always manipulate me with that. So I told him he could stay, but after Christmas was over he had to go. I was certain of that, no more! Through Christmas my heart was heavy, lost in my thoughts. I sat contemplating everything that had happened to me from as far back as I could remember, to the point I now found myself at...

Chapter Two

My fourth birthday...I jump out of my new bed, we moved house the day before, from Liverpool to Runcorn, so everything's new. Our house is a dorma bungalow; it's on a new estate in the middle of nowhere. All the red brick houses are pretty similar, some bungalows others houses, all had the same red brick estate look. Surrounding the estate is woods and fields and not much else. My new bedroom is down stairs next to my brothers, it's all white bare walls at the moment, and my parent's room is upstairs. I dash to the front door, to see if the postman had delivered my cards. Yipee!! I was delighted to see some yellow and pink envelopes sitting there on the mat. I knew they were mine; it's what always happens on someone's birthday. The cards are always on the mat. I scooped them up and dashed up the stairs to mummy and daddy's room. I'm so excited; I jumped on their huge bed, with its purple throw-over hanging off the edges, showing them my cards. Daddy put his hand down the side of the bed and pulled up my present. A beautiful brown rabbit teddy bear, she has a brown flowery dress on and cradles her baby in her arms. I'm going to call her Miss Rabbit, I love her! She's still with me to this day.

I'm seven years old, my brothers and I are going on a caravan holiday with my dad's family, my Nan, lots of aunties and my cousins. We all pile into dad's brown Nissan, ten of us squeeze together on the back seat, all shoving each other round. My brothers and I have never been away before, I'm excited. I sit amongst the madness singing with the radio - *'I'm in the mood for dancing...'* (1) The holiday is full of us all playing, my cousin fell off the roundabout, and my brother wants to go home. We climb trees, we go on walks, and we pile back into the car and go home.

I have two older brothers; James the eldest - five years older than me, and Anthony two years older. We have all inherited that Spanish look from my mum, her mother was Spanish, and each of us has black hair, brown eyes, and olive skin. James and I have wiry hair. Anthony is curly like my father. My brothers are always off in their own world with their friends. I play with the other children, riding my bike, making mud-pie's, and climbing trees. Proper little girl I am!! I did have woods at the back of my home to be played in.

My mum has been sick; she went to hospital whilst we went on holiday. Since we got home she spends all her time in bed, we all have to help look after her. Our dad is always in work and James is always doing the dinner or hanging the washing out. He looks so moody. Sometimes he looks happy, usually when his friends are around, now-and-then he makes me French toast, delicious! My brother is always up to something, once he brought a horse home. He knocked and my mum answered, to be greeted by a horse's head staring right at her on the door step. She screamed, we all laughed. He brought an injured bird home once too. He got caught stealing a bag of money from somewhere, poor kid got battered, I never did figure out what happened. He set his coat on fire jumping over a bomb fire, he got pushed off a twenty-foot wall. Always up to something! He was like a dad to me when I was young, he was the one who made me feel safe, I always adored him, and I always knew he loved me.

I'm nearly eight years old; my two younger cousins have come to stay. Their mum has some things to sort out so they are staying all summer holidays at our house. Jay is 6, his sister Shey is 3. They are so annoying, and they don't play with me properly. Jay gets cross with me, said I'm bossing him round, he picks up a shovel and hits me in the face. It hurt! My dad shouted at him. Now I think he's even angrier at me. Shey swung our cat round and round by the tail, she said she heard someone say 'You can't swing a cat by the tail in here'..."And you can!!" Shey said. They are annoying; I can't wait for them to go home.

I'm remembering the day my dad left us. There I was playing in front of my house with my friends, I could hear my parents arguing, but was trying to pretend I couldn't. Next minute dad storms out, into his car and sped off down the road. I can still clearly see his blue Ford Escort driving fast away from me. When I walked into my home mum was crying, she told me to go back out to play. It took days for mum to tell me dad had left us, and that they were going to divorce. 'Oh yeah and by the way Jenny you have a little brother, he's two years old.' "What!!" We didn't see dad for a while, and when he did come he brought this little boy with him - Jay-jay. Not thinking how his other children were, just about playing happy families with a little boy we had never known. I was very young and I did not get the enormity of it all. I played with him. He was a funny little thing. He was so cute and small, with big bright eyes and a sweet little face. Jay-jay would sing his rendition of Buffalo Soldier to Anthony and me. He remained in my live for the remainder of my childhood; sadly, we drifted apart in adulthood. He now lives down South somewhere, happily with his wife and children I'm pleased to hear.

My first birthday after my father left I sat at our telephone table all day waiting for him to call me, to wish me Happy Birthday. Wondering why my cards had not been on the mat like always, instead left on the table for me to collect. Everything seemed different when he left, quieter, less violence. Somehow it felt sadder. He never made that call. It was then I realised he was never coming home.

As children Anthony and I played regardless of the situation, well I say play but I think he got all the fun. Once Anthony, his friend and me where playing Superman in his bedroom. He told me to get on his top bunk and fly off, he said they would catch me in the sheet they both held beneath me at either end. There I am on the tallest building about to jump and fly, I peer down at my safety net and leap with gusto...holy mother of god...I screamed as loud as a banshee. Anthony and his friend dropped the sheet as I jumped, we had no carpets so I landed on hard floor. I broke my shoulder, my brother laughed...he still does. It was Anthony who would notice I was sad sometimes and try to cheer me up. I would be sat on my bed, snuggled up in my pink duvet crying. He would come in and ask me what was wrong. "I miss dad" I would always reply. Anthony would find a pen, curl his thumb beneath his index finger and draw this duck face on his hand. Then he'd give me a little show with his squeaky duck voice. I'd sit up and tuck my knees tight into my chest to watch the show, laughing away at the silly duck man my brother had invented. Either that or we would be dancing around to D.I.V.O.R.C.E, oh and we did love a bit of Power of love. Mum would be playing these records, obviously feeling sad, but we'd see it as time for a dance. Anthony and I fought like cat and dog in our teenage years, both angry at the life we had been handed. Now-a-days he is one of my best friends, although he is and always will be a floater. A dandelion blowing in the wind! He drifts from one place to another, but generally comes knocking for some curry every blue-moon. The older we get the closer we become.

Sadly, my relationship with James is none existent, the product of a family not just broken, but shattered from its very core. The damage coming from such a violent, bitter household has repercussions that are difficult to put into words. Sometimes people find it easier not to see someone who reminds them of the harsh reality of the childhood they once lived. My eldest brother bore the brunt of all the badness my parents put upon us, the violence from our father, and the disruptive behaviour of our mother. It was him who would run away all the time. It was him my father hit the hardest. It was him who had to pick my mum up every time she fell. He had to become the man of the house before he was even able to be a man. I will love him for all my days, no matter where he is, and I wish him nothing but peace and happiness.

Occasionally, when I got a little older, I would enjoy my own company. The area around our home was surrounded by fields and woods, and I would take myself off on random walks. One specific place was a beautiful little field. There I would be meandering down the long country lane, admiring all the wild flowers, my unruly hair in two plaits swishing from side to side as I'd merrily skip along to my special place. I would approach the field and take a short-cut. I'd jump over the little stone wall into the bushes and come out around the corner from my intended destination. The field was always calm yet full of life, nature. The birds singing, the bees buzzing, the caterpillars that I loved to discover beneath the many leaves from the array of wild plants. In the spring time this part of the field and the true reason I loved it so very much were the Daffodils that would cover the length of all I could see like a carpet of yellow flowers. I would sit amongst those Daffodils and I would feel peaceful...I would feel like it would all be alright - somehow. It was here that I had my first taste of the spiritual path I would eventually take, of course my young self was incapable of comprehending this at a level of understanding something other than what it was - peace, and knowing. On my journey back home after I had felt that peaceful feeling I would hear this voice in my head tell me to keep smiling. So I would smile and run on home. Daffodils are by far my favourite flower, when I see them those feelings still come back, or perhaps it's just the memory that remains.

Whenever my father would hurt me, or cause issues in our house that feeling would come to me, and I would hear the friendly voice in my head tell me... 'It will all be alright!'

When I wasn't doing those things, then I would busy myself with the thing that is, and always will be my passion, reading, my escape from life. In our home we had a copy of a book I so wanted to read, I loved the feel and look of it. It's ageing red leather cover, gold embossed title, and dusty old smell – it was mysterious. The print was too small for me, so I continued reading my Heidi tales.

The day eventually came when I did read it, and it remains one of my favourite stories. A story that allowed me to dream of a life away from the one I was in. 'Great Expectations'.
And I dreamt...of a better life.

Some of the vague memories that I had flashing through my mind that Christmas was being hit with a belt - the stinging, burning feeling on my backside, wondering why daddy would hurt me so much. Sneaking into James bed at night when I would hear dad hitting my mum. One night I remember it went on for a long time, the constant shouting of an angry man to his frightened wife, the clashing of furniture as her body would fall to the ground, the smacking of flesh on flesh, and the screaming. We all lay in our beds feeling the pain of what was happening. In the morning when we woke mum was sitting on the couch, she had sunglasses on in some vain attempt to conceal her pain. But we knew - the sorrow etched across her battered face. That's some scary stuff to listen to in your own home...from your own parents. I had listened to the sound of his fist hitting her flesh over and over again. My parents scarred my childhood.

My father was the oldest boy of twelve siblings, they grew up in a rough neighbourhood and you could say my father learnt to be tough to get by, but I think he picked a lot of his aggression up from his own mother, an Irish woman whose own upbringing had been harsh and strict. They were the kind of family who had no issues hitting their children with belts. My father is just another story of the apple and the tree, where no one is willing to change that ravaging cycle of destruction. He became a violent, volatile, cheating husband, abusing my mum - verbally, emotionally and physically. And not just mum, we would all, at some point, fall prey to his violence. Constant fighting! Constant violence! The effect this has on young children is one that can last a lifetime. The after-effects are traumatic inflictions that influence the person you are going to become. Even at very rare points in time when my father was happy, there was violence, only happy violence, to us anyway. He loved the dubbed karate type movies, and a bit of Monkey Magic. He would make me and my brothers sit quietly and watch them. After it was over he was straight to the choptastic karate fights, he would beat my brothers up, playfully. I would always hang on till everyone was busy then jump on them, my dad would just pull me down and pin me to the floor. He'd laugh at my cheeky first kicks I would give to him or my brothers whilst they were preoccupied.

My mother was the youngest in her family. She was someone who had suffered through many tragedies in her life. Her own mother died when she was a baby, this was the catalyst of all her future pain. She had been shipped around from one family member to the next, never feeling like she belonged. Then she met and married my father, the man who would control and abuse her through-out their marriage. She had been very sick at one point and my father did nothing, he still left every day to go and be with his secret family. So my mum sort solace in the bottle.

She drank as soon as seven o'clock at night would come, those bottles of whisky or vodka would be hidden all over our home. In the wash basket beneath our dirty underwear would lay a bottle of vodka, or under the stairs would be hidden a bottle of whisky, or in her wardrobe, or where-ever she thought we wouldn't find them. Mum too would have rare moments of something resembling happiness, but they were rare and only when her own family would visit would I see it. So the drink got hold of my poor inflicted mum, who was the kind of drunk that would become brave and vicious, slurring vehemently at us. Telling us how much of a bastard my father was, how we didn't know what he had done. Her warped mind would have her believing we hadn't heard the goings on, or hadn't felt his wrath ourselves before. She would tell us how much we had all ruined her life, not the man she chose to forgive every time, the man she made us forgive every time, no it was us that had ruined her life. She was lost in her own world of self-pity, her children were never enough to shake her out of the depressed, despondent life she lived. Mum's drinking got out of hand when she divorced my father, we would all see her in states. Struggling to climb the stairs to her bed, urinating herself before she managed to get to the toilet, or passed out on the floor in a face full of her own vomit, it was horrible and sad. So I spent the majority of my childhood crying myself to sleep at night.

We struggled financially throughout every year of my young life. We never went anywhere or did anything together, accept this; once a year, before they divorced, we would get taken to Blackpool beach for a play in the sea and some sandy butties. We would look in the distance at the funfair and wish we could go, my father always said no, not once did we get taken. That was as good as we got.

Mum would sit in front of the television waiting for seven o'clock to come, dad was generally absent - and when he was at home we would all know about it. That was pre-divorce, after it we'd only see him on a Friday for a few hours. He'll waltz into our home like he was still in-charge, eating food and turning the TV over, I hated him. Yet my mum seemed to still love him, my mum had a distorted view of my father. She always wanted his attention no matter what. It always confused me.

There was positive influence on my young life, although not enough. My mum's family, good people. However, they were somewhat ostracised from our lives. Both my parents, I'm sure, did not want them to know what was going on. My Aunty and Uncle where a special part of my childhood, I would on occasion get too slept over at their house. Uncle Denis, a very tall friendly man, who was just like his dad. He would take me around the park with his dog, a golden Labrador who was allergic to grass, and buy me ice-creams. Aunty Grace had no children of her own at that time, she was one of those wonderfully motherly ladies, and she would make me feel wanted and special. Aunty Grace had a kind face, and soft voice. She would cuddle me and I would wish I could live with them. My greatest influence, and one that still influences me, was my Grandfather. A tall intelligent man with kind eyes and fuzzy grey hair, he wore white vests and would tuck his handkerchief into his shirt, that would be open enough buttons to reach into and always had stains on where he had dropped his dinner. There was something sophisticated in him, even in his dishevelled manner. I was his only Grand-daughter, and I always felt special to him. We all did, he was that kind of man. He would sit me on his knee and give me maths questions, telling me how clever I was when I would get the correct answer. He'd chat away to us all, and take us to buy too many sweets, which my mum would tell him off for. He also taught me to tell the time and tried to teach me to play chess, left that one to my brothers. He said I had no patience's for it. I still talk to him sometimes. I can still smell him sometimes too.

So a year or so after dad had left us, our broken family moved back to Liverpool, so mum could be near her family again. It became apparent dad had only moved us all up to Runcorn so he could have his affair without ever being caught. So we went to live in a flat in an old Victorian building, second floor up. The house was all high ceilings and big rooms. There was a large garden at the back, at the bottom of the garden Anthony and I found a bomb shelter. We turned it into our den, all candles and cobwebs, glorious! The pair of us didn't know anyone else so we stuck together, we'd go out on our bikes yearning for the smell of fern amongst the trees. The nearest we got was Sefton Park, we'd ride around it for hours or we would be scaring each other in the dark looming caves', that sit eerily beside the park. To a child these caves where the scariest place on earth.

We would push each other into the darkness or dare each other to go the furthest in. We both loved to go sliding down the slope of Fairy Glen, Fairy Glen with its mysterious tale of two young sweetheart ghosts that reunite every Valentine's Day at midnight. It's a little magical part of the park that I imagined fairies did live, an oasis of stepping stones with an enchanting little waterfall. The greens of the shrubs and the smell of the wild pretty flowers that grow vastly around give it a feel of wilderness tucked away in a small part of the big city. Then you can go beneath the bridge next to the stream and watch tadpoles and ducks swimming along in their own world. I would sit for hours trying to spot a fairy beneath the branches of the shrubs, whilst Anthony climbed the trees nearby.

I always watched other families, and I wondered if mine was different or did they all behave like this when no one else was around. I was never sure if I should trust anyone, I would wonder if the smile that people gave was as fake as the ones my parents used. At a young age I learnt how to steal, I would steal sweets and give them to my friends, telling them they were from my dad. I obviously wanted him to appear to be a nice dad, I obviously wanted my friends to think well of him. I struggled even more as a teenager. I had no real guidance, and no real love. I would use school as an escape to have fun, I enjoyed the feeling I got from making people laugh or fooling around. I would give my teachers stick for any reason I could, enjoying the buzz from everyone else laughing. And if I wasn't having fun I was fighting. I had a terrible temper. My hot-headedness and learnt behaviours of violence always ready and willing to strike.

My relationship with my father was fraught to say the least. He'd done nothing but hurt our family. Another day etched in my memory is one where he attacked everyone in our house. He barged through the door and whipped off the belt he had on, and began attacking Anthony with it. I jumped on his back to get him off my brother and my dad hurled his fist against my face, he knocked me out. He knocked me out. I was only a thirteen-year-old girl. He bust my nose right open. When I came to I had blood pouring all over me. He didn't care, and it didn't stop him. The barrage of violence continued. He attacked my mum too and then he threatened James...with a knife. Afterwards everyone knew I had been attacked, the bruises on my face were something you couldn't hide. After it was over I sat alone in my bedroom crying, and I heard that voice in my head that felt familiar, it said everything would be alright. As I heard it I felt like I was back in the daffodil field, it gave me that feeling, it brought a

tiny glimmer of peace to me. In today's world if that happened, I would have been removed from them, and my dad would have been charged, but back then it was different.
What kind of family do I live in?? I knew this was wrong. Yet my mum always convinced me to forgive him. For a long time, I did try. When she made me forgive him for this latest attack I knew she was doing it for her own gain. She manipulated me into believing he was sorry and that the entire thing was a mistake. The older I got the feistier I became. I stopped feeling scared of him after he had knocked me out. I saw him as a coward who hit those who couldn't protect themselves. After that event I changed. I became angry, deep inside. That anger would come out to anyone who dared say anything to me that made me feel threatened. I never wanted anyone to make me feel that afraid again. Part of my mind obviously believed that by standing up for myself to other people proved I wasn't scared of my father. I had a burning desire to not be afraid of him anymore. I felt like I was becoming stronger and would one day be capable of standing up to him, and I did. The older I got the braver I became. Any chance I would get I would remind him of things he had done wrong. He never drank or anything so he had no reason to forget his violent actions, but he did have a tendency to distort the truth, and I had a tendency to remind him of the exact truth. The older I became the less he could use violence to keep me in line.

One thing that was an absolute from as far back as I can recall, was that when the time came for me to have children, they would be loved and cared for with every ounce of my being. This is the reason I am the mum I am. I would go through it all again if it's what made me appreciate my family the way I do.

I learnt to steal from early on the things that I wanted. When you grow up on the tough streets of any city, with a family who pay no attention to what you are doing and you don't learn good honest values. You learn what you live. One day, aged sixteen, I had moved from sweets to clothes. There I was as bold as brass slipping on a pair of shorts in the changing room - which I had done many times, I would have just pulled my clothes over them and walked out - when low and behold the assistant opened the curtain. She had that "Your nicked" look on her face. "Bastard!!!"
The Police kindly escorted me to the Police station, as the good citizens they *obviously* are. I was detained in this cold stinking lonely cell, with just a wooden bench and graffiti on the wall to keep me company. There I sat

alone and scared fearing everything around me. That fear was multiplied tenfold when I heard his voice... my father. Mum sent him, in that instant I hated her - again. How could she, she knew what he would do to me. The officer guided me out of that cell, and into the reception, seeing all I had seen and being present among so many Police Officers at such a young age was a terrifying experience all of its own, without having to face him. He sat there stony faced - the Police Officer told me to sit next to my dad, he never looked at me once. I sat beside him on this wooden bench, trembling with sheer terror - but still I never seen it coming. BAM!!! He wacked me hard with the flat of his fist right on my nose, my eyes watered and my nose burnt. For a split second my pain was halted, finally I thought he would get in trouble for his behaviour. I brought my hands from my face to look at the police officer, expecting something, anything...nothing came. He turned away like the good citizen he was as if he'd seen nothing.
My pain returned - worse somehow!

No one asked me why, or any other question you would ask your young child if they had been arrested for stealing. What happened when I returned home was I got screamed at and sent on my way. Left to guide myself to a better place. That night as I reflected the events of the day, I knew I had to change the way I was going. I wanted more from life than the way it was now. I had been spending my time robbing clothes and partaking in smoking drugs with the other teenagers from the area, who each had their own bad story to tell. I felt comfortable around them, like they understood the life I had to live. I had a deep resonate feeling that I was meant for something different from this though and I wanted to change it. I never stole anything again, my days as a thief where behind me. I took myself to college and enrolled to do my A-level in English Literature, the thing I loved. Reading and writing. I started to study Martin Luther King Jnr. He had a dream and so did I.

As I sat there thinking about all this a funny memory popped into my head making me laugh still, at my ridiculousness. A friend and I went out to town one night, sneaked out probably. There I am in a sleek tight little black dress my friend had borrowed to me from her sister's wardrobe. I knew I looked hot, one guy definitely thought so. I'm dancing away on the dance floor in some club in the middle of town, this guy kept coming over dancing with me. At the end of the night he pulled me to the side and kissed me. I was delirious, he was tall, with bulging muscles and he appeared so confident. He was a twenty-eight-year-old black guy from Manchester, and I was a sucker for muscly guys. I was still sixteen but I told him I was nineteen. He took my number and said we should meet up. "Yeah sure" I'd said.

A few days later there he was sitting on Tunnel Road in his top of the range Mondeo waiting for me. As he caught sight of me he looked shocked, I didn't understand why at the time. I was only sixteen and very naive to this kind of thing. So I rock up there adorned in my finest...a black and purple ski-suit...yep I said it...a black and purple ski-suit. It was the early nineties and in Liverpool ski-suits where in fashion. Not the attire for meeting up with men though. To add insult to injury, my mum had bought me the wrong colour trainers to go with my gorgeous ski-suit and these ones I personally chose to wear...I cringe as I write it... where brown and yellow Reeboks.

Words fail me too!

There's this hot twenty-eight-year-old guy waiting for this hot nineteen-year-old girl to come and meet him...and he gets that. Me dolled up in my best attire! Black and purple ski-suit and brown and yellow Reebok trainers! I probably had a ciggie hanging out my gob too. Classy snizzle that kidda!
He drove me to Manchester and back, seriously, just there and back. He turned around at the Manchester junction and just brought me home. God bless him for the effort. I must have talked some serious sixteen-year-old nonsense all the way up there. He definitely thought "Not a chance am I being seen with her...IN THAT!" I remember getting out the car and thinking - "What the fuck was his problem!"

A year later everything changed for me. At the tender age of seventeen I fell in love. It all began on the number eighteen bus - well I had met him before, but never more than a glance and a smile.

So there I am... "Single please" I'd said to the driver.
I walk down the aisle looking for a seat, and oh my god!! This gorgeous boy was staring at me. WOW!!! To my amazement, I recognised him, Anthony's friend.
"Hi!" he said.
"Hiya Jack", I sheepishly smiled back.

I sat down on the seat in front of him, and we talked. He was gorgeous, he wasn't that tall but he had muscles in all the right places. He was an amateur boxer - I had already heard this about him - and you could tell by the definition in his body. He had cropped hair, and the sexiest green eyes, with long curly eyelashes, that sparkled with mischief. As I looked at him the lines around his eyes wrinkled whenever he spoke, telling me a story of a boy who had already lived a life time. I felt like those eyes could engrave his name on my soul. To top it off, he'd made me laugh. His stop came far too quickly, as he left I couldn't take my eyes off him. WOW!! That's all I was thinking. WOW!!

All that day and the following days all I could think about was him.
Next thing I knew, there he was, in my house, with Anthony. There in a little terrace house in a small corner of Liverpool sat the boy that would change my life. I couldn't disguise my joy at seeing him. We flirted a little and he went on his way. After that he always seemed to be around. We flirted continually, mostly with our eyes. It must have been obvious to people, particularly to one of our friends, JP - a psychology student. He sussed it long before the rest.

Just seeing Jack was amazing. I would be out and about, being with my friends, doing my college course and whatever else my seventeen-year-old self got up too. Nothing memorable I know that, I had given up trying to be a rebel. Whenever I would come home he would be there. I couldn't believe he appeared interested in me. Our eyes would meet as we stood in a room full of my brother's friends, it felt like I was glued to the spot. He really was the most beautiful thing I had ever seen.
One night, one Friday night, a night I can recall everything about. I had dressed for a party. Had my best little yellow top on, same jeans I always wore - only had one pair - and the silver shoes I'd borrowed off my friend. I thought I looked fantastic. I walked down the stairs - I didn't know he had come round - but there he was, all alone in my kitchen.

"Oh hello Jack" I said in some voice, trying to be all sexy and confident.
"Hello yourself Jenny, where you off to?" he inquired.
"A party!"
"What about you?"
"Town for a drink"
"Is your girlfriend going with you?" I bravely asked.
"I haven't got one" he retorted, with a twinkle in his eye...

"No one wants me" he said quizzically. I didn't know what came over me. I heard the words come out of my mouth before I could think...
"I'd have you", I declared, and winked at him. We both just looked at each other, neither of us sure what to say. Then Anthony walked in.
"Ready Jack?" he asked.
"Yep", Jack said. On his way out he gave me the most amazing smile.

Fate played a hand on that night. The party I attended was uneventful, and my mind was consumed with thoughts of Jack, so I left early. I was sitting alone watching television at home when a knock came at the door.
"Jack!" my delight and surprise hard to mask. There he stood at my front door looking all gorgeous.
"I forgot my trainers, I was hoping you would be home" he shyly stated.
"Come in, I'll get them for you", I gave them to him, and I knew, standing there, finally alone with him, something was going to happen. Those beautiful green eyes of his had me spellbound.
We chatted briefly and then he said, "I'd better go then."
"Don't you want to stay", gosh he makes me brave I thought. His smile said it all.
We both sat down, and chatted and giggled like the teenager's we once were.
"You know I fancy you Jenny", he smiled.
My heart was beating so fast. "I don't know, do you?"
"Yeah!!" he replied.
We just sat staring into each other's eyes, it was beautiful.
Then he leant in towards me and kissed me.
That first kiss was one my heart and soul will never forget. A beautiful kiss that was the start of true love, he touched my arms and kissed me so gently, yet so passionately. We gazed into each other's eyes as our lips first touched. My entire body melted. And that was it, right there, from that very first kiss. He had me. I was his and he was mine.

'The chemistry was crazy from the kick-off, neither one of us knew why!' (2)
Mary J Blige

After that the pair of us was inseparable. I had felt that presence within me when I first met him that this was how 'it would all be alright'. That childhood feeling I had that something was going to come and change the life I was living was him, was Jack. I felt righteous in my belief because now everything was alright just like I had felt it would be. Over time I forgot all those feelings I had once had, I was living my life without thought. I sat there recalling so many of those memories. These memories confused me so much when I looked upon the person that was present in our relationship now.

On one occasion, we were both at a party. Everyone was doing their thing so we drifted out for a walk, it was within the first few days of us getting together. We strolled through the empty streets in the small hours of the day, walking and talking about anything and everything. Two young souls who knew something special was going on between them. Something different, and wonderful. We stopped in the park for a little kiss, it was absolutely freezing and as the darkness and the trees where swishing around us Jack and I held each other close and a warmth surrounded us. A warmth in the atmosphere encompassed us, it was a beautiful moment of love. This was not a feeling I have ever managed to find with any other man, I knew it was special then, and I know it even more now. That kind of love is not found often within the span of a person's journey through life.

I was completely in awe of this boy who had wondered into my life, and loved me so intensely. He treated me like a princess, like I was the most amazing person on earth. He taught me things I never knew and showed me places I'd never seen. Jack would always offer to do things for me, never letting me pay for anything, never wanting me to be upset, always making me laugh. He wanted to look after me in every aspect of my life. Making sure I had eaten, that I was happy, and that no one was upsetting me. He would tell that I would never go without and no one was allowed to upset me now he was around. Every time I would set eyes on him the butterflies in my stomach danced a merry dance, and my heart would glow like a beacon. Warm and in-love! When he would knock on my front door after work, he was an apprentice electrician, I would know it was him and a smile would spread across my face as I would rush to open it. He made me feel on top of the world. Nothing in the world could affect me whilst I had him, nothing. With him I felt safe and complete; he fitted me like the missing part of me I hadn't even been aware was missing until I found him. It felt like our souls had known each other for an eternity, and had searched an eternity to find each other again. My life was enriched sharing it with him. He made me feel beautiful, and he believed in me when no one else ever had. All my life my family members had hurt me, my mum through her self-involvement and bitterness, my father through his violence, and my brothers had always lay the law down to me for they were older, and male, therefore superior. So I spent my youth battling against them in one turn or another, my feisty attitude never went down well. Jack was the first person to ever applaud my strength, he'd tell me 'if you were a man the world would be in trouble'. His belief and love gave me a sense of peace I had never before experienced. Our love was strong and passionate. We never got bored of each other. We challenged, completed and loved one another. Jack had a personality that would light up a room. He was loud and gregarious, one of those people that walk into a room and everyone knows they are there. He was full to the brim of intelligent facts, he was strong and brave, and his sense of humour was razor sharp. He loved drama and chaos, whilst I was a calmer character. We both had tempers but mine flared when pushed, his flared randomly. Jack was scruffy at home, the complete opposite of my cleanliness. We were opposites in so many things, yet so alike and well suited in others. We laughed together all the time. He always spoilt me...chocolates, teddy bears, clothes, meals out. Trips to Blackpool and Wales, I had never been anywhere, it was fantastic.

'There must be an angel playing with my heart'. (3) **Eurythmics**

We would lie together on the grass at night, and gaze at the sky. We would talk for hours about our lives, our dreams. Jack picked me up, and swung me around, "You're more beautiful than the stars Jennifer Smith!! I love you!" He would sing to me *'It must be love, love, love...soon as I wake up every night, every day...'* (4) He swore he would never let anyone hurt me again, that he would protect me forever. I believed him. I loved him.
He too had had his own share of difficultly in his childhood and together we finally found love, the thing all humans crave is the love of another person. He truly was an amazing individual. We would lark about and laugh so much my stomach would always hurt. Being with him was so fun and light hearted. He had a tough guy reputation - a little boxer. I didn't see that, I saw the man who was endlessly kind to his beloved Nan, his little sister and brother, and... to me.

After just a few months of us being together Jack's mum had an argument with his dad, and his mum took his sister and brother to stay at their Nan's. Jack came to stay at mine. He never left. His family sorted out their differences and went home, Jack stayed with me.

So for years that's the way things continued for us, happy and in love. We argued like anyone else, both of us were feisty characters. We'd be shouting at each other one minute and then next we would be locked in a passionate embrace. We lived in each other's pocket in my tiny box room, and we loved it. We'd get drunk together, we'd play together, we were happy. We decorated my bedroom at Christmas, we bought a kitten together. We took his sister, brother, and my younger brother to a caravan in Wales for a week, were every day was full of fun and laughter. We spent most of our time down by the river splashing around, watching our younger siblings having fun. Jack was enjoying throwing them all in the cold river. He loved his siblings and even though he loved living with me he missed seeing them every day. It was a wonderful holiday of Barbeques, fun and wine. We were a young couple with no real responsibility other than to each other. They were happy times in our relationship. It was these memories when our love was so strong and deep that made what was going on now so hard to understand.

When I was eighteen I left my family home, James had become unbearable and he would moan about Jack and I all the time, about our music, the food we ate, the rent we paid. My mum would then moan at me about this endless list. She'd call me down stairs, I would know she was drunk, it was past seven o'clock and I could hear it in her voice. She slurred viciously and endlessly at me about everything. How I was making her life difficult, how I was eighteen and should be more responsible. How she was sick of everything I did, the way I cleaned her house like we lived in a palace! 'We fucking don't so stop kidding yourself Jenny'. How she couldn't stand listening to me laugh all the time, how I was fooling myself if I thought life was good, blah blah blah... on and on she went. We argued and I called her a drunken mess, told her she never appreciated anything I ever did. She moaned at me for cleaning up, instead of thanking me for helping her. She moaned about the way I put the washing on the line, the way I ironed, or anything else I did when I was only trying to help. So we left, we went to stay with Jack's parents whilst we saved for our own home. My mum never even tried to stop me, she never once said that we could sort it out together, she just let me go. At that time in my life all that I could see from my mum was how much she had let me down. She had never been strong or tried to enjoy her life with us. The older I got and the more my life became as complex as hers I understood her more, but I could never understand why her children were not enough to assist her finding some happiness. I wasn't sad to leave I was pleased to remove myself from my childhood life. Starting a new one was exciting, especially since Jack was by my side. I never returned home after that.

'...from the moment I could talk I was ordered to listen...I have to go away...if they were right I'd agree but its them they know not me...' (5) **Cat Stevens**

Then one-night Jack and I were in a taxi, on our way home after a friend's engagement party. The night had been good, the pair of us were rather drunk, and we began arguing. We got kicked out of the taxi. There we stood in the middle of god-knows where, shouting at each other. The next thing I knew Jack picked me up by my arms, about two inches off the floor, and dropped me.

My ankle twisted under my foot and snapped. It hurt so much, and I could feel my foot swell in my shoe. I knew straight away it was broken. When Jack lifted me from the floor I was as white as a ghost. He took me to the hospital, my ankle had snapped right through.

I could not even look at him. Why?
He blamed the drink, and swore he hadn't meant to hurt me...and I forgave him.
My broken ankle is how the next event in my life transpired...

Chapter Three

A day came that would change me forever, a day for me, that was so amazing words cannot describe.
You take the cellophane off the box, take out the stick, pee on it and wait. The emotions full of fear and elation. I walked in that bathroom one person, I came out two. I looked at Jack and said those words, "I'm pregnant!!"...I cried. He cried.
Jack grabbed hold of me and we kept hugging each other, then repeating these words, "I can't believe it, I can't believe it".
"Jenny we're going to be a mummy and daddy; I love you so much!!"
"I love you too Jack, I'm so happy". We both were.

From the beginning he was thrilled. He was there on my first visit to the GP, when my pregnancy was confirmed. A few weeks later we sat in the waiting area of the Women's hospital, both young and unsure of the process. "Drink lots of water" the nurse had said. I sat watching the other more experienced mum's-to-be, they drank lots of water as they waited, so I did too. They called my name "Jennifer Smith", and we went in. They get you to lie down on the bed and they apply gel before they slide the ultrasound scanner over your stomach. We both cried as we saw our child's first scan, there he was, twelve and a half weeks pregnant and he looked like a baby. He was sucking his thumb; I couldn't believe it. I thought it would just be a blob on the screen. We walked out of there elated, we were both so excited. It was after this scan that we told people. It was a wonderful feeling to say "I'm pregnant".

Each day I felt the miracle growing inside me. It was the most beautiful feeling in the world to know that inside me my baby was living and growing. I loved him even before I met him. I knew from the very beginning that this was what I had always wanted, my own family to treasure. I felt what I'm sure lots of women feel...like this was what I was made for. My body was designed for this purpose.

On a rainy Saturday in November, when I was just twenty, and Jack twenty-two years old, we moved our white fridge, green and red striped bed, washing machine, second-hand couch and an old piano - which we had bought for sixty pounds - into our new home, our own home. I was pregnant, and I had a home of my own. My life was fantastic. The harsh times of my childhood were over, I was moving into adulthood very pleased with myself. Our first Christmas was memorable for all the right reasons. "Merry Christmas Jennifer, and a Merry Christmas to you too bump", that was the first sound of our first Christmas together in our new family home. We ate too much, laughed a lot, and sang a little.

'Snow is falling, all around us. Children playing, having fun...' (6)
Good times!!

We continued happily preparing for the arrival of our miracle. Jack decorated the nursery, all lovely blue and green farm animals. Whilst I sat fat and happy, watching my guy decorate our first child's bedroom. The checked blue pram, pine cot and all the many other things we had discovered a baby needs were bought and awaiting use. When he came he blessed the entire family with his very prompt appearance. Right on the EDD, expected date of delivery for those unaware of the terminology!

Francis Jones!

My labour had been long and I had taken any medication on offer. So all that I could recall about the actual birth, aside from the hours of pushing, is prodding him as he lay on my chest, and saying "He's squidgy isn't he", and I remember Jack holding his new born crying son with tears streaming down his face as he said "Hello my son, I'm your dad", and Francis stopped crying straight away.

It was a few hours later when I was alone in my hospital room and the medication had worn off. I had fallen asleep, and when I awoke, right before my eyes was a fishbowl with the most beautiful, beautiful sight I had ever seen. My son! I scooped him up into my arms and cried. I could not take my eyes off him. The feelings I had for my son where immense, he had been living inside me for nine months. Growing and developing. Now he was here with me in my arms. I felt quietness, stillness, peace and knowing. Like in the daffodil field only this was so much more intense, this filled me with feelings I had never experienced. My entire being was bonded to this little baby that lay in my arms. He was everything I was made for, everything I wanted and needed. The protection and love, the instant bond I felt to him was immense. He had a huge mop of dark brown hair and big round eyes. I checked his tiny fingers, and then his tiny toes. He was absolutely amazing, and he was mine, to protect and treasure, forever. I had been truly blessed.

This was by far the happiest I had ever felt in my life so far. I lived in a place of pure love. My son changed everything about me. The moment he came into my life the despair that had been instilled in my heart from childhood was removed, a despair I hadn't known I had felt until it was gone.

'I have never been in love like this before.' (7) Lauren Hill

My father and I had had a strained bit part relationship. He walked through the door of my room in the hospital with his partner. Looking delighted about meeting his grandson. When I saw Gail (his partner), I asked her to leave. This is the woman who had cheated with him behind my mother's back. She had always done everything she could to prevent me from having a relationship with my father. Back in my childhood days when I craved his attention, it was Gail who would tell me to get off my own father's knee that that was her place. It was Gail that showed me, as a young nine-year-old, the grave of my sister, a sister I had known nothing about. It was Gail that had told my father Anthony had called her names, the reason he came to our home that time and attacked us all. It was Gail who had anonymously called my mum many times to tell her where her husband was. This was not someone whose poisonous mind I was ever going to allow near my child.

He left with her, and from that day to this, my father and I have had no contact. From that day to my dying day it will remain that any small feeling I had left for him, left with him that day. I finally understood what loving your child was meant to be about, because it was asleep in my arms. My father could stick his fucked-upness up his arse. Not anywhere near my son, not ever!

This ending to our relationship had a mere fleeting effect on me. Francis was all that mattered to me now. In the weeks after his birth, I found myself visiting Church continually. I had felt a strong desire to 'Thank the Lord' for the precious gift he had bestowed upon me. I was absolutely blown away by the love I felt for him, by the miracle of life. He was the most amazing baby ever to bless the earth, in my unbiased opinion. My love and need to protect him grew day by day. I wanted him to know I adored him, and I showered him with affection...I still do, and will eternally!! When you grow up in an environment like I did, one where love and compassion did not dwell. You either go one way or the other, you become them, or you become the total opposite of them. I always knew I would treasure my own children; I always knew that. Here he was, ready to be treasured.

So yeah... life continued, happier than ever before. A family!

Jack loved Francis as much as I did. He would call from work to talk to him - a tiny baby. It was Jack that walked the boards on those sleepless nights, he sang to him all the time... *"Close your eyes, say a little prayer. The Monsters gone, we're all alone, and your Daddy's here. Beautiful, beautiful, beautiful... beautiful boy! Darling, darling, darling...darling..."* (8) John Lennon. He sang it to him constantly, and he would always shed a little tear. There was no denying he loved his son.

It was in this year that Jack made a decision to go down a path that would alter the course of *his* life. Forever! As a young family, we struggled somewhat for money, but I never even thought about it, or anything else for that matter. Everything became secondary to Francis for me, including Jack. Although I didn't even realise I wasn't giving Jack the attention he had previously had from me, but then Jack didn't give me a chance to settle in with my new important role - Mother!!

Jack had been chatting with a guy he knew, called Mr.Z. This guy offered him money to mind a van load of pot for the night. Easy money, someone delivers a van to you, you sit up all night and protect this van laden with drugs. The only reason being was that the lorry driver always came late at night, and their lock-up couldn't be entered until nine the next morning. He came home and revealed his plan to me.

"I don't like the sound of that Jack", I said.

"Babe I'm only sitting on it for a night, we'll get £300. We'll be able to do some things on the house, and its only pot." Jack replied.

Our house was new, and we were young, just starting out on our journey together. We had no carpets, and just a few bits of furniture. With a new baby, and so much expense it had become a struggle. I never gave it too much thought, other than a new carpet for Francis to crawl about on. Besides what harm could come from it, it was only pot.

It went on like that every couple of weeks Jack would disappear for the night. I stopped asking him where he was going. I enjoyed him being out the house so I could be alone with Francis. This went on for a few months, Jack going missing and then turning up with money. Off we would all pop to the supermarket to fill our cupboards, all our bills got paid on time, and of course we had our new carpets. After a while though Jack must of obviously had another chat with Mr.Z, because soon enough our kitchen was fitted out. I knew this was a lot more money than a few three hundred pounds now-and-then could accumulate to. But again, I didn't give it much thought, my obsession with Francis was the only thing on my mind.

Our first Christmas came, our first as a family. It was fantastic.
"Jack that tree won't fit in our house" I laughed, standing outside on the cold street, holding Francis in my arms shivering. We had searched for hours, wanting the best tree ever, for Francis's first Christmas.
"It will you'll see!!" he laughed. It didn't, but he made it, somehow. There were many presents laid out, we had a Christmas Express choo-chooing around beneath our humungous tree. Our house a merry wonderland!
"It's Christmas..." I blasted it loud for all to hear around six in the morning, my excitement too much to quash. I woke Francis from his sleep, eight month old Francis, just so I could see his face when he saw Santa had been. How naive, he didn't have a clue. I unwrapped the presents we had sat up all night wrapping. Francis played with a box.
We all had a wonderful day.
"Goodnight my sweet boy and Merry First Christmas!" I said as I kissed him asleep, the tears rolling down my face. I was so happy.

New Years was spent abroad visiting Jack's family. They all went off into the night to see in the New Year. Jack, Francis and I stayed at home. There we were all lying in the bed together, Francis asleep on his daddy's chest, me by his side.
As the fireworks exploded...I felt a completely profound happiness resting in my heart. Life could not get any better. I had everything I could ever need right here with me forever.
But...he was obviously thinking something else.
A few weeks later he obliterated my heart into a million pieces.

How blind had I been!!

Jack had begun going out all the time, telling me it was the nature of his job. I blindly accepted this tale, until one-night Jack came home to inform me of what he was about to do.
"I need some space".
"I don't understand, what's going on? You need space from what?"

I replied.

"Jen I'm still only twenty-three, I've got a mortgage, and a family...it's too much".

We argued, I tried to understand, but couldn't.

"Is it someone else Jack?" I fearfully asked.

"No, no, it's just...I need some space", he looked me in the eye and knew he had to say something more.

"You don't even see me anymore Jen, you just see our son. I'm not jealous, I love that you love him so much...but I have needs too!!" he shouted.

"You can't leave us, we're a family" the tears streaming down my face, my heart on a one-way track to demolition.

"It's only for a while, till I sort my head out..." he said this ever so, and turned on his heels and left.

'The first cut is the deepest.' **PP. Arnold**

That night, the first night was one of the longest, hardest nights of my life. I lay in my bed all alone, with endless tears rolling down my face. I thought they would never stop. Never before had I experienced pain like it. In the pit of my stomach sat a heavy weight and my chest felt physically sore, it was as if Jack had stuck his hand inside my chest and ripped out my heart, stamped all over it and then stuffed it back in. The enduring ache slowly killing me. I adored this man I had always envisaged us hand in hand, an old married couple walking down Blackpool Prom. I literally felt my heart repeatedly implode with every second that passed by, as I realising the man I loved didn't love me anymore, it hurt so much I felt like I could die. The lightness he had given my heart when we had first fallen in love was replaced by this heavy broken ten tonne ticking bomb. I couldn't grasp how he could hurt me like this. I still couldn't see the obvious thing staring me in the face. In the following days every part of me felt crushed beyond repair. I didn't eat, I didn't sleep. I cried, and I smoked. At first I even struggled to get up and do what I needed to do for Francis. How could I come to terms and understand how one-minute I had been so happy, the next I was in so much pain. The man that had made my world complete, had now destroyed it.

"How could he leave us?"

He would come around to our home like everything was going to be alright. Jack would pick Francis up and take him out. I cried the entirety of them being away from me. I could not get my head around how I had been in such a happy state one minute, to then be engulfed in this pain the next. I had thought we were both happy, I was wrong. Turns out Jack had been very unhappy, and had required something to alleviate his troubled mind.

I found the answer to what Jack had used to assist in his struggle. It came in the image of a fat girl, wearing blue eye-liner and not much else. This girl kindly left dead flowers on my door step, along with a nice graphic letter telling me where and when she had slept with Jack. I have to tell you the anger that I had not felt since I had first fell in love with Jack all those years ago returned vehemently. I am a hot tempered girl and I flew into a rage, I wanted to hurt this girl, who I believed was responsible for all my pain. This girl had taken Jack from me and didn't even care about the pain she had caused. If I had got my hands on her at that time she would have been in hospital and I would have been in a Police Station. Thankfully I never found her, the girl stayed as far away as she could, for as long as she could.

Turns out Jack could not allow me to devote all my time to our new born son. My conclusion was that men are only happy in a relationship when the sex is constant. I realised that men had no depth, no emotion other than the one in their pants. He had been seeing this girl behind my back for months, lying and deceiving me. I had been betrayed, and fooled by Jack, and by all the other people that knew and never told me, some of these people I had known for years. So it hurt when I realise they would have sat and gossiped about something that hurt me so much. The entire event triggered something in me from childhood, distrust. I began to distrust everyone, again. My whole world had had the rug well and truly pulled from beneath it, I felt alone and weak. Our relationship had always been such a beautiful thing, and his betrayal made a mockery of that. My feelings were scattered all over the place, all those stages of 'grief' that set in. Denial, anger, frustration, desperation, loneliness...pain! Then a distrust of everything I thought I had known.

Weak though is not in my make-up. It just refuses to dwell in my soul, I guess because it made me feel like my mother, and that's not who I am. I had a son to stay strong for, the only thing that assisted me coming to terms with such betrayal, and to make me smile again. Francis was my saviour through this trauma, his love made me strong. One day when Jack

brought Francis home after he had taken him out, I was sat on the couch as Jack handed a nine month old Francis back to me. As Jack turned and left, I felt the emotion in the depths of my stomach rise. I tried to keep it together. I didn't want Francis to see me cry. A solitary tear rolled down my face, and my sweet baby crawled right in close to me and wiped away that tear. I hugged him tight.
I refused to be defeated by Jack's betrayal, so I enrolled at college, and took myself to the gym. I was still sad and my heart was still in pieces, but I plodded onwards. I am a positive person, and I told myself I would never let anyone defeat me. I would never allow anyone to turn me into my mother.

'You gotta be bad! You gotta be bold! You gotta be wiser! You gotta be hard! You gotta be tough! You gotta be stronger!' (10) **Des'ree**

Jack soon wanted me back. Although this was not my intention, but he did! I had missed him and the love we shared. My life had felt cold without him, like a part of me was missing when he wasn't beside me. My heart didn't feel that burning existence he gave it when he was with me. Jack had a hold on me that was true. It was what Jane Eyre had felt about Mr. Rochester. He was the *first* one to ever *see* me, and the *first* one to ever *Love* me. So I forgave him.
The first night we spent back together my passion for the man I loved over rid the reality of my emotions.

*'Take the ribbon from my hair, shake it loose and let it fall......
help me make it through the night...I don't care what's right or wrong, and I won't try to understand...'* (11) **Gladys Knight**

After the initial euphoria of having my true love back had subsided reality kicked in, and getting back with him brought something I was unprepared for. Something I couldn't talk to anyone about. I had thought I could forgive and forget, but as he kissed me I realised how hard that would be. When his lips touched mine and his hands touched my body all I could visualise was him touching and kissing her. In the pit of my stomach that pain I had first felt, that initial pain, returned. It lingered there like bad breath shouting 'he done this with her'. It messed with my head, a lot! The aftermath of my heartbreak, to have been with someone for as long as I had been with Jack, to have felt we were meant to be together forever, to have shared every ounce of myself with him, have that snatched away and replaced by this negative gut retching feeling... that words cannot truly describe. Sometimes I just wanted to punch him in the face when he would kiss me because my mind would just be picturing them. I hoped it would pass, but when it was happening I struggled. How can you give yourself, intimately, to someone when you feel like that? Unless you're a man. Men don't seem to need to feel close to a woman to give themselves to her. Women do though. We need to feel that connection. This had a really adverse effect on me, and I know he could feel that too. The trust had gone and with it went the intimate closeness we had previously shared.

"It's the worst mistake of my life Jenny, and I'm so sorry", his words full of remorse, his actions over time showed a different story. He had gotten deeper into his job of 'choice', and his personality had changed. The strength he had once loved in me was gone in his eyes, a strong woman wouldn't have forgiven him, and his ego knew this. His ego fed off that glimmer of weakness he seen in my soul. My strength of character would still rear its head when he would try to deceive me or play me for a fool and his ego needed to put that down, he begun to hate something he had once loved about me, then he learnt how to manipulate me. I had fallen in love with a beautiful man, and now I was faced with another side to this man, one who could be an arrogant, obnoxious individual. He would say all the things he thought I wanted to hear, but the sincerity of his words was gone. Money changes people, and generally not for the better. Every day was different, we could have days of goodness, and then days of badness, the reality of living with such a complex individual. One who was the man I fell in love with one minute, the next this man I didn't recognise. Within the complexities of our relationship we still shared a deep bond, we still spend time together, laughing and loving. We shared a love of food, so our thing was meals out. Beautiful nights spend eating wonderful food, and drinking fine wine. Nights I would have the man I loved beside me, the man who made me feel warm and loved, instead of the man other people had begun to see. But those times began to drift further and further apart.

My heart loved the man he once was, and I believed he was still that man, beneath all his bravado. Being a child of a broken home I wanted my son to have what I never. A complete family unit, confused, confused, confused..."why was life so difficult!!" At points in our lives after his betrayal, are relationship was toxic, at other times it was all that it had the potential to be, the couple we had it in us to be. Jack had a unique ability with me, he always had the ability to make me laugh. I'm one of those people who need to find humour in the direst of situations. I know this is a form of defence from childhood, but it's in me, I can't change that. And Jack always made me laugh. I suppose it's how he melted the ice that surrounded me when I was mad at him.

We continued on this path for a long time. I thought this was the reality of life. That I needed to accept people make mistakes and that this was what life had dealt me. I just got on with taking care of Francis, and enjoyed Jack when I could. Francis and I got to do so many things, things I hadn't thought we could do. I had my own car, and I would take Francis off on adventures to where ever we wanted to go. We would go to the safari park and pretend to be in Africa amongst the animals.

"Watch out Francis there's a lion behind us!"
"Quick mummy quick let's move outta here"

We spent all our time together, he was a beautiful funny little soul. He always made me smile. He would look up at me with his beautiful big brown eyes. Francis made my life happy, nothing else mattered. Nothing made me happier than him. I adored watching his every move, his every milestone, big or small. We would go to his play groups, go swimming, or the park. He would do dances or little funny scenes to entertain anyone that came in our house. I would drive him to the beach and make sand castles, or visit real castles. He would pretend to be the king or a strong brave knight. Francis loved it, no matter what we did, he loved it. He was such a happy child. Together we travelled on many holidays, Barbados, Menorca, Portugal, Holland and Spain. We travelled around Ireland, seeing all the beautiful green landscape, the mountains and the wonderful greener than green hills, that show why it's called the emerald isle. All the monuments the place had to a troubled background, monuments that stood randomly in places that some atrocity or other had occurred. I loved our holidays together, we would be a normal loving family. There would be reminders of his life back home when he would take me in shops that stunk of pretentious bullshit, which it would be a lie to say I didn't enjoy. Once upon a time it was not even in my imagination to be able to afford to shop in such shops. I knew what he was up to, where the money came from but I never asked him. I believed the less I asked the less involved that made me.

On our way to another holiday as I sat in the airport I was sure I was pregnant again. I rushed into Boots and bought a test. Our call to board

the plane came before I got a chance to take it. As we buckled up I leant over to Jack and said "I think I'm pregnant!"
"Really?"
"Yeah, I've just bought a test from Boots."
"Go do it then let's find out" He replied excitedly. When the seat belt sign went off I popped into the toilet, I came out slid back into my seat and just smiled at Jack. Our holiday was wonderful, just the three off us. When we returned home we told everyone I was pregnant again. I was really happy.

Our lives at that point were full of holidays. Two months later I was back on a plane over to Spain, this time with Jack's family and Francis. Jack was staying at home. One night I felt really unwell, I put it down to the heat affecting me whilst I was pregnant. I took myself to bed early, in the middle of the night I woke with excruciating cramps in my stomach. When I got up I could feel the blood and I knew straight away. My heart sank, and all I wanted was Jack. I tried to call him but he didn't answer. I took myself to the hospital, I was alone and afraid. This Spanish doctor kept trying to say things to me that I didn't understand until he said the only thing he knew in English to explain to me what had happened.
"No baby! No baby!"
"What...I don't understand...I'm pregnant." My eyes no longer able to stop the tears, I sat in that white sterile room amongst strangers crying.
"No baby...no more!" he said.

I walked out and called Jack, who was a lot more interested in his friend than he was about me. He didn't seem that worried.
"They probably got it wrong" he nonchalantly said to me.
"I'm bleeding Jack" I cried down the phone.
"Jen come home then, and we'll go the hospital here!" So I booked onto the next flight back to England. This was something that was not to be. In the hospital that I knew, they confirmed I had miscarried. They said the baby had stopped growing at eight weeks and I was still in the process of miscarrying. They took me into theatre to remove what was left. It was all rather traumatic and distressing. I grieved for my little lost baby, but somewhere deep inside I told myself it just wasn't meant to be.

Not long after this Jack flew me to Paris. Sitting on the plane on the journey over he pulled out a ring and asked me to marry him.
"I never want to lose you Jennifer Smith. I have been a fool risking losing

you before, and now I just want you to be my wife."
I said "Yes."
It was all rather romantic and I was completely swept away with it. We flew into Charles de Gaulle airport and straight into a taxi. As we drove into Paris central I was shocked how condensed the traffic was, they did not take any notice of the lanes. They would squeeze into any available space. They all drove fast and dangerous; I admit I was rather fearful. As we came to the Champs Elysees through the Arc De Triomphe we pulled up at our hotel. We got out and a porter came straight over to help us with our luggage. The hotel was very elegant. Outside was all opulently structured plants and a French flag draping down from the pole. Our room had a view of The Arc De Triomphe.

Jack surprised me with a meal in the Jules Verne, the restaurant within the Eifel Tower. As we walked towards the entrance, which is a separate doorway with its blue and gold paisley rug laid out, and the usher in his Tuxedo waiting behind his tall speaker table, his reservation list at the ready. Some of the tourist visiting the Eifel Tower where trying to get a table at this exclusive restaurant. They were politely told if they didn't have a reservation they could not dine at the Jules Verne. Jack walked straight up to the host and said "We have a reservation, Jack Jones"
"Ah yes Sir, right this way." he ushered us in towards another attendant near a lift. So we walked in and Jack gave me a cheeky grin.
"When did you book this?" I asked.
"I told you I was going to surprise you Jen!"
In the restaurant our waiter guided us over to a table near the window looking out on the River Seine, he explained the French menu to us. The only thing I understood was' filet de boeuf'. Our waiter was an old white haired guy dressed in a very sophisticated suit, he was friendly and helpful. He could see we had never been here before. He explained the entire menu to us. He even suggested we must return in July when the Sun sets on the River Seine, as it was the most beautiful. We told him we had just got engaged and he gave us a complementary glass of Champagne. When we left Jack took me into a Boutique de chocolat, the most beautiful chocolate shop ever. It was very elegant, all the chocolates where displayed behind a glass counter in gold, red, silver and green tinfoil wrappers. A row of exquisite boxes, tied gracefully with delicate ribbon lined the table running through the middle of the shop. Jack bought me a very luxurious box of chocolates, and we left. We went back to our hotel and made love all night.

The following day Jack and I walked around the very romantic streets of Paris, all cobbles and historical buildings. There were old fountains and little nooks around every corner. Lovers walking hand in hand, embracing the most romantic city in the world. You still encounter beggars on street corners, and tacky stalls selling mini Eifel Towers and other souvenirs that had been made in China, even in Paris. We stopped every so often for coffee or a patisserie.
The day after we went shopping in the posh street, lined with Haute Couture. Dior, Gucci, Prada. Jack bought a pair of Gucci shoes, and I bought a beautiful black embellished Dior clutch bag, and an elegant pink silk and lace underwear set, all wrapped in tissue paper and boxed up before putting the contents into a bag. The most memorable and romantic thing we done though, out of all the things we did was sitting on the Champs Elysees eating a sandwich. We sat outside under an umbrella watching the Parisians go about their lives in the rain, and it was one of the most romantic memories I have of our relationship.

So when we returned home I bought a dress, ordered flowers, sorted a venue, made sitting arrangements, the wedding was on...but all we seemed to do was fight.

Jack would go out drinking, not all the time, but often enough. He would go out partying, coming home with cocaine swirling through his body. He would either be violent and destructive, or gurning and incoherent. Or not come home at all. On those nights I would lay awake in my bed in a state of paranoia; my mind would conjure up all kinds of images. All of which brought a heavy weight into my chest, and a sickness in the depth of my stomach. I imagined every scenario, him laughing with other women, talking, kissing, touching...him sharing himself with other women when he was meant to save that part of himself just for me. My heart told me I was right, but I could never prove it, for he had become a master manipulator. Jack would often disappear, sometimes for days and days. I would accuse him of cheating, I couldn't believe the falsity of his words. He would say it was business, or that he had been stressed and needed a 'blow-out'. When he'd come home he would often smell like he'd just gotten out of a shower, this spurred on my paranoia. I knew he had showered because the smell of his actions would catch him out. He'd take his phone everywhere with him, where ever he went in the house that phone was with him. He'd dress to impress, stinking of aftershave, when he was supposedly going out with his friends. I would quiz him about who he was going out with, and would try and trip him up the next day, always trying to catch him out. He'd convince me I was paranoid my mind began to believe him, my heart shouting "No!!" I did not know how to listen. "The up's and down's", my naive mind told me. Too many people around me at that time were living the same sort of existence. Your man goes out on benders, you argue, you get back together. Normal life issues I let myself foolishly believe. At this point in my life our relationship was awful, I was behaving like Miss-fucking-Maple trying to catch him out. Feeling like it was what I needed to end it. Proof that he was cheating like I stupidly needed a reason to end it, when the reality was I was scared to stand alone. And he was behaving like Pablo-fucking-Montana, selling drugs and then sticking his nose in a heap of cocaine, his narcissism taking over his being.

The arguments got too much and we split up again. The wedding got cancelled, and he moved out. I became accustomed to this life of mine. The pain wasn't as intense as that first cut, so I coped. Then we got back together, again. We played this messed up dance with each other for too long, he didn't want me, but he didn't want anyone else to have me, and I wanted the man I use to know. On more occasions than I want to admit he became violent towards me, it was not often, but once is too often. I was not an angel either, violence was within us both.

The worst time was New York, the last time before New York was this. We had gone out together to a wedding reception with Jack's co-workers and their girlfriends one night, big glitzy night that's all about what you are wearing and what present you have bought. I'm dressed in a very expensive silver metallic Mui-Mui suit I had bought in Paris. I don't go in for all the heavy make-up and false nails. I curled my hair and put on some mascara, bit of lip gloss and I was ready to go. This was something I very rarely took part in. I didn't really like the company of many of the girls or his friends. Most of them treated other people terribly, like the way they would click their fingers at waiters or look down their nose at people who weren't dressed in the right clothes, forgetting exactly where they had come from. Or in some cases where their dad's had come from, some of them where just spoilt little rich kids whose daddy had provided their way into the life they lived. Most of them were very pretentious people. I had my own friends and wasn't keen to join their circle. Jack had promised me he wouldn't touch drugs at all and was very insistent I come along, and that we would have a nice night. I was sitting with the girls having a chat,

whilst he was with the boys. Next thing it's late and we're all dancing away when someone comes up to me and says "Is that your fella?" In my heart I wanted to say "no" but he was at the bar making a scene. I was pissed off seeing him like that. He had obviously been taking something. As I walked over, one of his friends joined me.
"Nights over Jack, time to go home." His friend told him. He slurred something and thankfully made no objection. We got in a taxi and went home. As we walked in our house I took off my high heels rubbing my sore feet.
"What the fuck are you doing?" Jack shouted
"We're going back now!"
"Jack the nights over everyone's gone home" I tried to stay calm because I knew how easy he could turn when he was in such a state.

He swayed his way into the living room saying he was making a call then we were going back out. He couldn't find his phone, he'd dropped it on the way in the house and I had it. I turned it off and stuffed it in a coat near the door, hoping without it he couldn't get hold of anyone and it would deter his desire to go back out. I went to walk up the stairs just as he came back into the hallway, and he grabbed me by my hair.
"We're going out now put those fucking shoes on!"
"I'm not going anywhere Jack now fucking get off me"
He dragged my head up and then smashed it on the floor. He smacked me in the face as my head bounced off the floor. Then he strolled back into the kitchen like nothing had happened, mumbling something. I was sick of this, but in that moment I was very afraid of him. That blazing look in his eye had come to scare me. I knew if he would just sleep I could leave him and end this when he was sober in the morning. He would always proclaim to not remember anything in the morning, and I was sick of going over his disgusting behaviour with him. So to prove my point I did something I was afraid to do, but something I needed to. I knew my video camera was sitting on our kitchen table, so I went in and turned it on, turning it towards him whilst he mumbled incoherently to himself. He shouted at me "Where the fuck are you going" as I went to walk out the kitchen.
I was calm, and I knew the camera was on him. "You've just hit me Jack, again!"
"So fucking what, you deserve it. Fucking slag!"
"I'm going the toilet" I said as I left the room. The camera rolled recording

all his horrible drugged up state. He fell asleep eventually. The following morning, I packed some things for Francis and me and put them in my car.

I put the camera with a note next to him for when he woke up. This time he could see for himself what he turned into when he stuck that crap up his nose. When he called me the next day, I didn't answer. I'd taken Francis to my friends and wasn't sure what to do next. I never answered the phone for a few days, leaving him to worry about us. When I did answer, he cried down the phone and told me how ashamed he felt. He said he had watched the video and it was the worst thing he had ever seen. He swore he would never touch anything again. After a few days of his constant begging for forgiveness I relented and went home, he sat me down and gave me the sorry routine. Looking at me with those vulnerable eyes, telling me how he hadn't dealt with the many issues from his own childhood. How he had watched his own father attacking his mother, and how what he had done to me he had witnessed his father do to his mother. Jack's mum was just a worn down defeated woman, who had only wanted a normal family, but instead she got stuck with Jack Senior. Jack's dad who Jack had many issues with, his dad had always neglected Jack as a son, and Jack had always tried to appease him and gain respect from him. Jack Senior had been just twenty when Jack's mum had fallen pregnant with him, and Jack knew he was never wanted. Not by his dad anyway. He was a man who enjoyed the power he had over everyone, especially Jack. His ego was full to combustion when he felt powerful. He had a typical small man, egoistical, macho attitude. He ruled with an iron fist. In-fact the definition of a psychopath explains Jack Senior best, he is ruthless and calculating, he does not know the difference between right and wrong, he lies to justify his own actions, empathy and remorse of any kind evades him, he actually believes the lies he tells to justify his actions in his own head. He is highly manipulative and has no consideration of anyone's feelings but his own. The older Jack got the more he became a threat to his dad. His dad would be-little him and physically attack him if Jack in anyway done something he deemed as worthy of such treatment. He once tried to bite Jack's ear off, his own son. He even attacked him one day by throwing him into the garden and booting him with steal toe-cap boots on, just because Jack had borrowed his shoes. Jack Senior knew how to mask his true self with a smile to those that didn't really know him, his charm all superficial and controlled to suit. He inflicted Jack's soul deeply. As Jack got older his dad developed a new strategy to remain in control. His relationship with his dad always concerned me. It was actually the catalyst behind Jack's entire life decisions.

Again I fell for Jack's tale of woe. Somewhere inside me I pitied him. I understood the damage watching and living with that violence could do to a person, and I had witnessed first-hand the repercussions of Jack's father's actions to know the damage he inflicted. After that he never touched anything, until New York.
I wasn't one for going out drinking and partying, I preferred spending all my time with Francis. I did however always observe the events around me. At that point in my life I struggled to comprehend the extent of the devastating ramifications hidden behind their narcissistic glamorised enjoyment.

I remembered my first time seeing the sights of Marbella. It's main attraction I was on my way to see, Puerto Banus, tucked away. There I am walking down the road with a few other people, looking for all that I had heard about, but everything looked no different to other parts of Spain I had seen. The variety of shops selling summer clothes, bikinis, swim suits and inflatable crocodiles, the white apartments with verandas and colourful shades. Then you walk around a corner into this Port, it's like you have walked into another world. That's when I first clapped eyes on this old leather looking man with three mobiles phones in his hands, and a young blonde titty type lady, dripping off his arm. There parked up around the port is an array of Ferrari's, yellow ones, red ones, black sleek sports cars with their top down. There is a multitude of swanky yachts moored up around the port; most of them are bigger than houses. Some had come from countries far, far away, whose owner's wealth exceeds all of Liverpool put together. I watch a woman in a navy blue poker dot swim suit, wearing an oversized straw hat, relaxing casually on her lounger on the deck of her yacht. She sips away on a glass of ice tea, pretending to read the newspaper, whilst really watching the passers-by admire her wealth. There are shops selling watches and handbags at prices people could feed a family for a year. Glass tanks full of live lobsters sitting idly outside restaurants waiting for customers who desire to eat them. The glitz and glamour of such a place is a mask for the superficial dark world that is controlled by money and power and is hidden behind the paper thin facade. Were where these people from, they sit on their luxury yachts looking down upon you like pheasants. Jezz!! If the old adage of little-willy's and their big toys is anything to go by, there are some serious maggots in Marbella.

That summer there we were, again, holidaying in Spain, something that had become the norm a regular trip to Marbella. One night we were sitting at a table in some posh seafood Restaurant right on the beach, I sat at the table looking out at the sea as everyone began arriving. We were about to eat with a few other people, all in 'That World', everyone was chatting away as they took their seats. These people are the kind of people who generally only mix in their own circles, they live and breathe the same kind of existence. The things they say and do are acceptable and justified. The level of notoriety they emit, the respect they command and receive from those around them is astonishing to watch. They are like rock stars in a fucked up world, then again I imagine rock stars' worlds are pretty fucked up. Sat around the table you have Joe, who is slobbering over the bread, olives and oils the waiter has placed on the table. His name is apt as he's the image of Joe Pesci. I've been banned from telling him this as he gets offended and goes on endlessly when someone offends him, spitting venomous aggression at whoever dared disrespect him. Unless it's a man and then he would just knock them out. He laughs like Roger Rabbit, and I am desperate to say something humorous, but I've been warned to keep my comments to myself on these nights. Joe has this psycho look about him, you can see in his sullen grey eyes every thought he thinks is nasty, yet he thinks he's God's gift. He always has an array of different women, always ends in murder, and it's always her fault. Tonight he's alone. His latest conquest had to go because she wouldn't bend over enough for him, his words. I can't understand what anyone sees in him, he's a bald, ostentatious midget, who slobbers over his food like a pig and laughs like 'wahayhayhayhay....', it's vile. He's vile! Obviously the money's enough for some. Then you have the Irish guy, Aiden, around 5ft 10, about forty years old. It's the first time I have ever met him, although I've heard a lot about him. He's built like a brick. He's definitely been on the steroids. He's all platinum teeth, tanned skin and muscles, hair perfected styled. He talks really quietly, but has an air about him that shouldn't be underestimated. I see him smile at comments said at the other end of the table. You just know he's collating everything anyone's saying for analysis later on. He has an understated watch on his arm that has been mentioned before and cost him forty-five grand. His wife is a brunette with a killer body. They both obviously enjoy the gym. She is elegant and reserved, she doesn't say much all night. Her name's Gwen.

Then you have the old guy, Andy, about fifty-eight, over 6ft tall. He has white hair and is heavy built, not in a fat way. You can see he's strong and capable. He also has really soft, gentle sky blue eyes, and an enchanting smile. If it wasn't for the two-inch gold bracelet dangling off his wrist, and the sovereigns on his fingers, you would think he was a sweet old guy, he's the one I'm sitting next to. I've known him for a while now. I'm even comfortable cracking some little jokes about the crazy midget at the other end of the table. Andy likes my sense of humour and we get on. His pride about his children is massively convoluted. He is regaling me with a few stories since I last saw him, about his son Barry. "He got nicked for robbing the jewellery shop, ran in with a gun, got off on a motor bike. Police chased them. He's been told to make sure his drivers are good but he never listens to me. Buzzies caught him. He's in nick now, but we'll get him out." He's gregarious and talks to me for hours, right little gossiper he is. He has spent the majority of his life in jail. A real street kid, so poor he didn't have shoes sometimes when he was growing up. Quickly learnt his size and bravery could help him survive, and earn him money. He got in with a man when he was fifteen who killed people for a living. He worked for him doing odd errands, knocking people out, or beating them up when killing them was too much. He learnt this drug-dealer trade from that man's contacts, they all earned huge amounts of money together for years. I understood the mentality of survival that comes from those streets. It's do or die! You want something; take it, because you aren't going to get it any other way. Trust no one! You become someone who is never free to be more than the person you're made to be. His wife is next to him she's one of those wives who know they live a good life and likes everyone else to know they live a good life. Pauline, same age as Andy, childhood sweethearts they are. She has platinum blonde hair, and gold and diamonds dripping off her. I can hear her telling Gwen what designer dress she has on, and where she got it. You can always tell Andy is proud Pauline can say those things, he's proud of the life he has given his family. He sees his stints in jail as part and parcel, a bit of rest time. They are a rare couple who actually really love each other. Then there is Paul, early thirties slightly smaller than Andy, he has a belly on him, everything he wears is Hugo Boss. This is Jack's buddy out of this group. You can see he over-indulges in everything. Drink, food, drugs, women. He talks about himself none stop, the kind of guy who never really hears anyone else talk. He's flamboyant and has a rakish air about him. I already know he cheats on his wife I have seen him many times before with other women. He brings his wife out one night and his girlfriend the next. His wife,

Shanice, is a crazy woman. She swears and smokes like a trouper. I've heard she beats these women up if she catches them with her man. She talks loudly across the table about catching him with some other woman, like it's the woman's fault, and he just smiles apologetically. And finally the big guy, Peter, he's not the tallest out of them, Andy is. He's about 5ft 10, strong build and very physically fit, he's around forty-five. He has sexy enticing big brown come to bed eyes that I am sure most women find hard to resist. I am positive if he got me alone I'd be fucked. He has this old-fashioned vibe about him. He is alluring, highly intelligent and personable. He laughs when something's funny. He talks when he has something to say. He listens to what everyone else is saying. He is without doubt the authority in this group. He isn't married and his girlfriend's back in Liverpool. All of these people sit around the table drinking fine wine and amazing food, talking loud and laughing like any average group of friends. Only these aren't your average people and their conversations range from how well they understand the stock market, to nonchalantly regaling in congratulatory tales of deception and violence. Underneath the pretend comradeship you think exists among those individuals who were sat at that table is a level of competition and jealousy in each of them. Except for Peter, he is at the top of the ladder. The confidence of his mind projects through his body language. He views himself as the 'God of Gods'.

All these men talk about their other co-workers with code names, like 'minge one' and 'minge two' or the 'the horse 'or some other nonsense name they give each other - although I'm sure my names suited them better, like...'Tommy two tits' or 'Nobless Bob'. They continuously discuss the ten boxes of t-shirts or whatever blatant bullshit terminology they use for selling drugs. How it made it to its destination or how it didn't. Who's getting what, who owes what. All egotistical money-men, that are so easy to recognise, and Jack was one of them. When you walk around, you see them everywhere. It's not just the flash car they drive or expensive cut of their jeans, their shoes and the Rolex on their arm that gives them away. It's that swagger they have, that cocky, arrogant attitude that emanates from them. "I'm loaded and respected, you're just a dickhead going to work to earn less money in a year than I earn in a week". They think women are a purchase they make, there to do what they want for them, when they want it. They believe that they are cleverer than everyone else because they earn so much money. When in reality, beneath their money and power the majority of them do not possess any attributes that could assist in their evolutionary progress. Depth of character evades them, which shows their true intelligence is minuscule. Although they are not alone in that process, far too many individuals put a judgement on success based on their intellect and the money they earn.

What a world eh! It was bizarre, but indirectly I had become a part of it. Although there was so much I didn't like about being within its environment, it would be a lie if I denied my material inclinations where not swayed by the luxurious exquisite things I could now afford to buy. I was the kid at the back of the shop whilst everyone else bought sweets, the one who wore her mum's tops and her brother's jeans. On the rare occasions we had money to buy a bar of chocolate, my brothers would ask for the eighteen pence mars bar, but I always wanted that twenty-three pence fruit and nut, my mum always said I had expensive taste. Of course I was swayed, I could afford all the fruit and nuts I wanted now. Also I enjoyed meeting *some* of these people. Whether you agree with their existence or not, there are interesting stories amongst them. Stories of a life you can't understand unless you have lived in it, stories were people had to do things to survive, and sometimes those things escalated to a point of no return.

'Street life, it's the only life I know.' (12) **Randy Crawford**

What a fucked-up world I had gotten involved in. One it was apparent I had I learnt to accept. Then one day, a few months before Christmas, Jack surprised me with a trip to New York.

Chapter Four

Back from New York...

Christmas came and went, and then Jack left, off to his mother's, again!

It was an exceptionally difficult time over the Christmas period, barely a word passed between us. I was glad when it was over and he left. All my pondering was over. I knew our love had been true once, but I had to accept that the life he lived now changed him, and that change in him polluted the love he had for me. In all honesty it had never been the same since that first cut. I just wasn't capable of accepting that before, now I had to. I believed that was it, that Francis and I would be making a new life for ourselves.

Life though does not always go the way you think it will. Surprises wait around unexpected corners. A few weeks later I discovered I was pregnant. Ironically, New York had been one of our worst times and one of the most beautiful times we had shared, and before Jack destroyed it, I had fallen pregnant. Another miracle to bless my life.

With the latest tragic event Jack had put into our relationship, it made me feel like I was being pushed into a life I never thought I would allow myself to live. My heart was so confused, again. I had once loved this man. He had been so good for me...once. The man that stood before me now however was not the same man. He had become some kind of Jekyll and Hyde character. One minute he was funny and charming, loving and caring. He was generous to his friends and his family. He looked after my mum, was generous to my brothers. He loved his son. He played with his son, and gave him everything both of us as children had never had. He loved me too. I was that young girl who had melted his heart. The girl he would do anything for, the girl he wanted to look after for the rest of his life. The girl he thought was more beautiful than the stars. This man made me feel happy and alive. This was the man I loved. The next minute he was aggressive and horrible. Cunning and manipulative, behaving like he was better than other people - because he earned so much money. He had become a man who controlled his girlfriend, and I had let him. A man who took cocaine and became violent, he hurt me physically and emotionally. He was changing into some dark being before my very eyes, I watched something beautiful turn into something ugly. Narsacism took over him and the bigger his ego became, the more he unconsciously took away my personality. The strength of his ego took control of our lives and the bigger it became the weaker I unconsciously became. This man made me feel afraid, and it made me wonder who exactly I was, because I was beginning to forget. I hated that man. He blamed the stress of his job, the job he chose. How it had many pitfalls; like forever knowing people were only interested in what you could do for them financially, having to be responsible for other people's money, watching your back for police or worse the people you thought where friends that were willing to grass on you for their own security. At the time I obviously fell for this load of crap. What I now realise, after so much reflection is that life is not something that can be defined with easy answers, or step by step guides. No one's journey is the same, and no one's reaction is the same to any given situation. I could say I was naive or whatever but the truth is I was afraid to stand alone; afraid I couldn't cope. I had become completely dependent on him and I was afraid to remove myself from the only man I thought would ever love me, the only man I thought I would ever love. The man who was the father of my children.

'I'd rather live in his world than without him in mine.' (13) **Gladys Knight**

The love I had once felt for him ran so deep I felt I couldn't live my life without him, even though my love for him was now so distorted. Then, I couldn't see the wood for the trees. My deep rooted childhood afflictions also had me yearning for a solid family unit. As much as I had hated the pain my father brought to my childhood family, I had strangely missed having a father once he was gone. As a child it had hurt to watch other children with their fathers and not have my own. I did not want that for my children. I suppose I thought I had to fix things with Jack, like somehow I could make this work. Like I had the ability to bring back the Jack I had fallen in love with, the Jack I knew was capable of being an amazing dad.
Even though my life felt confusing, the elation at being pregnant was again immense. I relished being a mother. I always felt it was my destiny. We had both wished for this child, there in St. Patricks Cathedral, we had both wanted him or her. So I made the decision to put the past behind us, and try again. Obviously it was far from easy, we had many long discussions before I relented and took him back. It took me a lot longer to get over it.

Sadly, this was in no way like my first pregnancy. It was a time of contempt and immense stress. The contempt was from me to Jack, for obvious reasons. To be honest I was a nightmare to live with, I was moody and irrational. I had become insular once again, not discussing how I truly felt about anything. My unhappiness in the life I was living was evident. I hated what I believed at that time *he* had made me become. The stress was from an event that was the beginning of his down-fall.

Some months into my pregnancy, something happened. To this day I still don't know exactly what that was. All I do know is mass amounts of drugs were involved, and whatever it was it went wrong. When this occurs, threats and violence follow. This is how things started from my viewpoint.

There I was sitting at home on the couch, after a long day running around after Francis. When I heard the key in the door and Jack walked through our hallway into the living room, he looked seriously furious about something.

"What's going on Jack?"
"Jen, look...I'm sorry about this but..." a long pause followed "...something's happened, and we're gonna have to go away for a while", he tried to sound calm, but I could sense I should be worried.
"Why, what the fuck's going on Jack?" I demanded.
"Look you're not going to like this but...I gotta be honest with you. I've been doing some business with these Cockney's and it's all fucked-up".
"What do you mean Jack?" the fear in my voice evident.
"Babe I don't want to go in to all the details, but listen...me and the boys will sort it out. It's just...they...erm..."
"What Jack, What???" I shouted.
"They've threatened to hurt you, or someone...to hurt me".
"What!!!" Shock began seeping through my veins at what he just said.
"I'm pregnant, we have a little boy. What are you playing at?"
"Jen...Babe...I'm sorry...I..." he didn't get to finish. I stormed upstairs.

We had to pack some bags and go, Francis thought it was another holiday and excitedly packed his toys into his little Toy Story suitcase. The first night we stayed in a hotel in town, the next night we drove to Wales and stayed in another hotel. In the coming days it filtered through that these people where extremely dangerous, the kind who got off on dishing out violence of the worst kind, the kind of men who have no compassion for the life of human beings at all. They would hurt men, women, they had no preference. These men wanted to hurt me or someone in Jack's family. Their threats were serious and they were dangerous. People I didn't know wanted to hurt one of us because Jack and his co-workers had done something, something that they deemed worthy enough of hurting the people he loved. To say I was afraid is a huge understatement. I know I should have run as far away from Jack as possible, but I was deeply fearful.

We spent weeks travelling around England. Staying in hotels and renting cottages. We spent large amounts of time in the Lake District. It was such a refreshing change from the city we both knew. Moving from one place to another though is not the ideal scenario for a pregnant woman and her young son. Jack was constantly trying to appease me, going out of his way to keep me sweet. His manner was one of someone who actually loved his girl, when the truth was his new found love for me was all built on fear. He knew I was deeply troubled, and that he was on the verge of losing us. Truth is I would have left him then if I could, but I was petrified. 'What if someone tried to hurt my son or me?' I was safer with him than without him. I felt vulnerable and in desperate need to have him by my side. My warped mind was also enjoying his attention. I enjoyed us being his focal point, not having to share him with his co-workers or his friends. Some messed up part of me enjoyed being in control, finally having him listening to me. He had to, he had no way of getting away from me, and he couldn't go out on benders whilst we were living like this. So we played a new dance, one where he feared losing his family and his business. One where, as far as his family was concerned, I held all the cards.

Sometime over the summer it all got sorted out. How? I had no idea how. Did I ask? No! I again chose, consciously, to remain ignorant. I felt uncomfortable knowing some of the things you become privy to in that bizarre world. I knew he would never take us home unless we were safe. So Francis and I finally went off home, Jack too...our relationship hanging by a thread. It was now based on our son and our child to be. Nothing at all to do with two people in love, the essential thing needed to have a happy relationship.

I sat watching the TV one Tuesday morning, heavily pregnant, with just two weeks to go. I was shocked at seeing what was being broadcast on every channel...

An aeroplane had collided into the North Tower of the Twin Towers. The World Trade Centre that we had eaten in just nine months before. I had gotten pregnant there, and I was awaiting my gift from New York to make an appearance. Somehow I felt connected to the place. As with every other person that was watching it, I was horrified, scared and completely shocked. What a tragic event.

Just eighteen days later and eight days overdue, my second miracle presented himself to me, a beautiful little boy. He was my 'Fairytale in New York', the baby we had wished for in St. Patrick's Cathedral.

Joseph Jones!

'I'm the lucky one, came in eighteen to one.... I love you baby...this year for me and you...I can see a better time where all our dreams come true...' (14)
The Pogues

Joseph came into the world screaming; louder than any baby I had ever heard. His birth was quick and easy, compared to Francis'. Joseph had some mucus on his chest so we were both taken to a ward. People arrived before I had even had chance to have a shower. Francis of course, Jack's mum, and James. It all happened so quickly. My head felt like it was going to explode. I rushed to the bathroom and vomited. After a while everyone went home, and although it was lovely having them there I felt relieved when they had gone. I pulled the curtain around my cubicle in an attempt to remove the exterior distractions. I scooped Joseph up from out of his fishbowl and his crying stopped, straight away. He had come into this world, eight days overdue; he came like a tornado in the blink of an eye. It was as though he hadn't wanted to be parted from his mummy's womb. He'd obviously been comfortable in there, and now he screamed until I had him in my arms. Then he would lay there all content, like all he wanted was to be with his mummy. We lay on the bed together, Joseph staring contently up me, me gazing adoringly down at my beautiful new son.

This was the boy that was going to test me and love me in ridiculous quantities. When I had slept with him that first night in the hospital I knew I had been blessed yet again. I was as obsessed with him as much as I had been with Francis. I would lift Joseph up to the sky and all his skin on the top of his head would wrinkle, it was so cute, it was as if he had too much skin for his head. I'd sit with him and Francis crying, I felt so blessed.

Again Jack was a fantastic dad, he would sit and rock him, sing to him. Drive him around and around in the car, the only thing that would get him to sleep. Joseph though was not the passive happy baby Francis had been. This one had a voice with a top rate volume and he used it, frequently. Francis was so happy with his new brother and would ask me to put him in his arms so he could look at him. Francis was only four years old, I would sit him on the couch with loads of pillows and place Joseph on him. My tiny boy sitting on our big brown leather couch, surrounded by all purple and pink pillows, his big brown eyes looking at me, his little baby brother asleep on his knees. It was so cute. He would try and play with him; he thought I had only had a baby so he had someone to play with. It felt amazing to have two beautiful sons. My childhood had affected me greatly; it was in the love I felt for my children that I understood how bad my childhood had been. How lacking in love our family was.

Jack and I tried to rekindle our lost love, and on some occasions I would feel tinges of that love. Like the night before I gave birth to Joseph, I had been so fed up and emotional. Jack put Francis in his mum's over-night and took me for something to eat. We chatted and had a little giggle, it all felt relatively normal. The following morning when my waters broke Jack cleaned it up, helped me get ready and took me to hospital. We were the same bonded couple we had been when we had Francis. The two of us doing it together. He is good in the labour room, he helped me to stay focused and calm. In those moments our love for each other was still evident.

Christmas came about all too quickly. We bought our tree, decorated our home, laid presents beneath the tree and eagerly awaited Santa's visit. Our family was becoming bigger and this gave Christmas more magic than ever. It was actually a pleasant time. Things felt alright between Jack and me. We were now parents to two children who make it impossible to not be excited at Christmas, when children are amongst you Christmas is always full of magic. After New Year had come and gone Jack informed me he was to go away for a few days.
"Where are you going?" I asked.
"Jen I'll be gone a few days, less said the better eh" he replied.

Generally, over the years I had come to enjoy those times when he was not at home. It could be like living in the midst of a hurricane living with him. I would enjoy it being peaceful and calm, doing whatever I wanted without him disturbing it. Strangely, this time, I missed him, immensely! When Jack called me one night, he said he was feeling the same. Something felt strange. He said he couldn't stop thinking about me, and that he had been dreaming of me. He had said he was missing me more than he ever had. There was some undetected thing between us that neither of us understood. It would be years later when I looked back on this situation that I would realise. The feeling we had was a foreboding one. He returned two days later.

That night as we lay in our bed together, there was this feeling between us. We just lay there in each other's arms, no words passing between us. In moments like that words are not necessary. We lay in the silence looking at each other, remembering the love we had for each other. We made love like it was the first time, like it was all new...or like it was the last!

As events would have it, it was...

Chapter Five

It was a cold Friday morning in January and I was woken by the sound of the phone ringing. As I stretched over the bed and picked it up, I didn't recognise the voice on the other end, and he didn't introduce himself.
"Get everything out your house!"
"What, who is this?" I sleepily asked.
"Just listen, get *everything* out your house, ok!" This man said with a demanding tone, and then he just put the phone down. I was startled and confused, who was that, and what did he mean? Jack was not home he had gone somewhere the night before and not returned. I tried to call Jack to see if he knew what it was about. Jack didn't answer his phone, so I decided to sort Francis out for school and then I would try him again. So I put the phone back in its place and got up out of my bed.

I walked into Francis' room, smiling adoringly at my little Angel sleeping. "Francis wakey, wakey! Time for school!" Francis stretched and yawned, his big brown eyes peeking out from under his heavy sleepy eyelids, then he put his arms around my neck and pulled me towards him for a snuggle. We got up and ate our breakfast, got dressed and then I walked Francis to school. We chatted all the way as usual, Francis holding the side of Joseph's pram. I kissed him goodbye at the school door, Francis kissed his brother, or he tried to, he got slobbered on instead.
As I walked home I wondered who that had been on the phone, and what he had meant. 'Get what out of my house?' I felt quite fatigued, little Joseph was only four months old, still having night feeds and I was feeling the demands of that. I opened my front door with its wonderfully coloured glass panels, took off my coat, hung it on the rack in the hallway and contemplated a nice cup of tea. A bang on the front door startled me, making me jump. As I turned I could see through the glass in the door that there were several people standing on the other side. I opened it apprehensively, as I did so, all those people aggressively walked forward into my house. There was about eight of them, men and women. Before I got a chance to speak one of them said these words;

"Jennifer Smith, we are from Customs and Excise and we have a warrant to search this property. We have Mr. Jack Jones under arrest on suspicion of importing class A drugs..."

That same person continued saying whatever it was he was saying, but I didn't hear anything else. I was shell-shocked. I couldn't even think. My mind was a complete blank. They all just walked into my home, like it was their own, and began searching. Through all the kitchen cupboards, behind the couch, under the stairs, through the books on my bookcase, even in Joseph's pram, everywhere!
Suddenly I realised I could hear a baby crying amongst the muffled voices as they ransacked my home. It took me a few minutes to register it was my baby, crying in his pram, surrounded by strange faces and hearing strange voices. I picked him up and held him tight in my arms, as if he could somehow remove the event playing out in front of me. I held him all day long, feeling some sense of safety by having him so close to me. Joseph has his father's beautiful green eyes and they looked at me, filling me with comfort.

I could not leave my house all day. They searched through everything. They found money in a shoe box under the stairs, and also a hand gun under the mattress in my bedroom. More Police came, armed Police Officers. They had their *own* armoury saddled into their bullet proof vest, one of them stood in the door way of my bedroom for hours. My house was over crowded with Police, and Customs Officers. The day was long, draining and exceptionally complicated. They keep asking me questions, each one I answered - "I don't know". I was too busy asking myself questions; why was there a gun in my home? What am I going to tell Francis? How had this happened? How had I not seen this coming? Why had I not stopped this from happening?

I discovered that not only had they been watching Jack for several months, and that when he had gone away a few days prior, he had gone to Northern Cyprus, which they suspected was to buy and arrange a shipment of drugs. They had followed him the night before, and arrested him and three other men after observing them meet some Dutch lorry driver in some dark shady street to collect several holdall bags. They had then loaded their cars with these bags and zigzagged up the motorway. These bags had contained huge amounts of heroin, and they had taken them on to a hotel. This is where they had arrested them, somewhere close to London, in some hotel, in the middle of the night. With heroin... heroin! I couldn't believe that's what he had gotten into. The drug even most drug dealers wouldn't get involved with, it's seen as being touched by the devil. Jack was involved though, and it appeared he was tangled up more than I could ever imagine. I didn't even know he had gone to Cyprus! I guess I should have asked him what he was up too...

That first night Jack's mum came to my house, she was obviously devastated. She had had a few drinks and cried all night. We also had a visit from a person called Laurel. He ever so tactfully (not!!), sat around my kitchen table with Jack's mum and me, informing us that Jack would go to prison for twenty years. He was perfidiously emphatic about the entire situation. Declaring his help whenever needed. I could already see in his eyes the lies and pretence; he was trying to play me like a fool. The father of my children, the man I had fought against all odds to stay with, would be gone, almost completely from our children's lives. It didn't matter what anyone said, the cold hard truth of it was, he was gone. After everything I had been through with Jack, all the effort I had put in to staying together for our family. Now he had been removed regardless.

That night I didn't sleep, I didn't even cry...I just lay there dazed, confused and lost. A few days later a story about it was spread across our local newspaper, everyone in our area knew about it. They talked under their breath as I would pass them in the street, or at the school. They would look at me like I was something they had scraped off their shoe. They obviously thought it bothered me, it didn't. I was never interested in what others thought of me. Some mothers stopped their children playing with my son, this did bother me. Surely they were not that ignorant to assume he was in any way at fault, he was four years old for goodness sake. They didn't see that; they saw a family they assumed were drug-dealing scum bags. A misconception formed in the minds of their own ignorant, inexperienced, judgemental attitudes.

Jack was moved within days up to a prison in Liverpool. That's when I got to visit him for the first time. My first experience of a prison was as abysmal as you can imagine.
I got in my car and drove towards the prison, parked up and entered the reception. I sat in the waiting room, full of all different kinds of people. Some of their children sang "Jail time, jail time!" Their mothers sat clumped together with their friends laughing at their children's song. 'Oh how funny!'
What! What the fuck! What world had I just walked in to?
"Visits for Jack Jones" they shouted.
"Put your finger on there", one of the prison wardens ordered, I pressed

my finger onto this finger print analysis machine. Then they marched me and a few others through several locked huge doors, into another area. "Take off your shoes, belt, and jacket. Put them in the tray and walk through the metal detector". A female officer patted me all over. "Remove your bobble!" I wondered why? I soon discovered. People will hide drugs in any place they can to smuggle them in. In their hair, in the waist band of their clothes, even stuffed in a condom and slotted into their nether regions or in a condom in their throat ready to regurgitate it into the mouth of their invitee. Anywhere they could, in any way they could. Then the visitors are made to stand in a line whilst the sniffer dog walks by smelling everyone, if he sits down you don't get in. I entered this enormous room that was full of other prisoners and their visitors. Prison wardens scattered about in different places. Huge amounts of tables and chairs all spaced out symmetrically, all chairs were moulded to the tables, and each table had one green chair - for the prisoner. All manner of people where there; arsonists, rapists, thieves, drug addicts, drug dealers, murderers, paedophiles, all getting visits from someone - I felt sick. I walked to the desk, as did the others, and was told where to sit. As I sat waiting my heart felt like it would explode if it continued to beat this fast. I caught sight of Jack coming towards me, and then there he was sat right in front of me. The only words I can recall from that conversation where "I'm sorry Jen, I'm so sorry..."

I had been a stone cold individual who had not shown emotion from the point of those Customs Officers knocking on my front door. But when I left, and got back in my car, I put the key in the ignition and BOOM!!! Like a tidal wave my emotions erupted... the tears came. I cried for what felt like an eternity. I cried for my children, for myself, and for Jack. Eventually I got myself together, dusted myself off and drove home.

A Single-Mother!

A decision I made on that drive home back to my children was; now that it had become just us, me and my children, and the father-figure I had so desperately yearned for had gone. I knew I needed to be the best mother I possibly could be. I would give them everything I had to give.

In the months that followed I lived on auto-pilot. My only concern was taking care of my sons, and keeping it together. I hardly ate and I couldn't sleep, I could barely think straight.

Francis missed his dad so much, even though Jack and I had had a

turbulent time, my boy and his daddy where close.
I struggled to explain, and I lied constantly.
"Daddy's had to go away to work", I blamed the war in Iraq, said his dad had to make machinery for the soldiers, said the Government made him go. I did not want to tell him the truth. I believed the bitterest truth would affect him more than my lies. Not a chance on earth would my son's ever be singing "Jail time!"
I also missed Jack so much, I know life with him hadn't been good over the last few years, but we had been together since we were young, he had always been around me and the heart does what it does. Who has the power to change that? You can't control the heart it doesn't listen to logic.

I struggled to come to terms with the situation I was in. Everyone around me was sad, and I witnessed all of their pain, as well as carrying my own. Each individual family had to deal with the court case - one long day after another, one court then another. One set of issues, then another.
Listening to the politics of each individual's desire to get away with what they had done - Jack was not the only person arrested, and each of them had their own agenda. Putting someone in a situation of this magnitude will always show you the true strength of their character, generally the person perceived as strong in their "big fish little pond" world, are the weakest, and most vulnerable. Each other individual involved had their own case and their own families dealing with the devastating impact of the impending situation. Each different intricate level of this issue was continually bringing problems to my door. People who wanted me to find them assistance with whatever it was they, in some corner of their mind, believed I could possibly help with.
Visiting solicitors and listening to legal terminology was becoming part of my everyday life. I despised it. The obvious traumatic emotional feelings of having to visit a prison, and taking my beautiful sons into such a dire place devastated me each time. All the issues of everyone else involved and our own family issues cooked up a recipe for a desperate predicament.

Whilst all this went on I felt stuck in the centre of a nightmare I didn't belong in, one I couldn't wake up from. I was sick of hearing legal jargon, of listening to everybody's endless opinion on what was going to happen. People discussed things matter-of-factly. Forgetting or realistically not caring that for me - it was 'my life'. Anger became my new best friend. My view on everything was distorted and naive. I was trying to be this perfect mother at home and the stress was having an enormous effect on me. I was angry at everyone and I took my pain out on other people. I would argue with people for no reason, road rage, shop rage, people in general would bear the brunt of my aggression as I uncontrollably needed to release my anger. I shouldn't have, and it was not my intention. Yet again in my life I couldn't get a grip of my emotions.

It was the summer nights when I really felt lonely. I did not want an array of people around the house when the boys were in bed and I would have visited people in the day, and done all I needed to do. So when night came and the sun was still out, I would be at home, alone! Twenty-five years old and this was my situation. I would sit in my garden smoking, listening to the variety of other people enjoying their lives, the neighbours putting dishes away after they had eaten their meal together. A man's voice telling a joke and the woman he is with laughing, the everyday clatter of family and friends spending time together. The many different normal existences that I was listening to going on around me, I sat there trying to make sense of everything that was going on in my own life. Nothing was making any sense though...I was lost.

When I would go out and return home from where-ever I had been, I would sit in my car scared to face my front door. I would get an aching heaviness right in my heart. I'd get out of the car and stare at the door. It was one of the hardest parts of being in the situation I was in. I would look at the door and know no one was inside to welcome me. I'd stand there for a few seconds struggling to accept the enormity of what I was feeling. Eventually I would put the key in the lock and turn it, then inhale deeply before fully opening the door, preparing myself to be greeted with quiet loneliness. No one was home; the house was empty and solitary. In the winter I felt the cold that waits behind the door. In the summer it was stuffy and stale, no fresh air, no life inside. Behind the front door, inside my home, I could ignore some of the harshest realities. I would feel safe in my home with my son's, as long as we had each other I was alright. Faced with the door, I could not!

The pain just kept coming - when my boys would do something special.
"Francis you are amazing...."
"Joseph you walked...."
First steps, first bike ride, when they made me laugh with their ingenious

whit, and I would look to tell someone, yearn to share what I had witnessed with someone, that someone should have been their father. But no one was there.
By far the worst pain I struggled to deal with was the grief Francis felt. Holding him in my arms whilst he cried for his daddy tore me apart.
"I want daddy; I miss him..."
My little boy who was only five years of age, I had wanted to protect him from everything, yet he was feeling pain words could not express. He was an innocent bystander in the entire sad situation. He had not done anything to deserve the pain he felt he was an angel from above.

The final day in court came towards the end of the year. I had showered and dressed before the boys woke up, nerves swirled around and around in my stomach. My friend arrived to mind the boys and I set off. Everyone's family where there gathered outside the court room chatting amongst themselves, awaiting entrance. You walk into a room full of varnished wooden furnishings. The Judges seat is a raised bench where everything else is facing towards it. The seat is a green leather and mahogany wooden throne like chair designed to intimidate. The Judge however only comes out of their Judges chamber when everyone else is seated and quiet. The barristers sat behind the tables directly in front the Judges seat, all adorned in their white wigs and black gowns, their desk has stacked up evidential paperwork, and some of it was splayed out in front of them ready to use. The solicitor or legal secretary sat beside them. I watched Jack's barrister whose wig was tilted to the side and wondered if he knew this and it was some rebellion on the uniform he must wear, or was it a mistake? Then the rest of the people were sat along the rows of pews in the public gallery. Jack had admitted conspiring to supply drugs, but they had no proof of conspiring to import and that charge had been dropped months before. They all sat awaiting their fate, dealt from a person none of them knew. Jack looked over at me, he mouthed "don't cry" to me and smiled apologetically, he knew me that well even from a distance he could see I was already on the verge of tears. The four people, including Jack who had been arrested on that January night sat in the dock. A reddish brown enamelled wooden oblong box area with a pew firmly screwed to the back, wrought iron caging surrounding the box, a warden stood in the corner. The dock was situated just close enough to the Judges bench to hear them speak when asked to. We all sat watching, listening. All of them had had talks with their own barristers before-hand, all of them had some idea what was about to happen. All of them had admitted their part in the situation, which instantly lessened their sentence. As they had admitted involvement there was no trial, it went straight to sentencing. The three others got their sentence, five years, six years, and seven years. Jack was portrayed as the ring leader of these four and he was up last.

"Jack Jones you have admitted your part in supplying Class A drugs, you have no previous criminal convictions and you attest that this was the first time you have been involved in such criminal matters. As you have already admitted your part in this, you are guilty as charged and I sentence you to ten years' imprisonment." Jack looked at me and smiled, like this was a blessing. He knew he could have gotten so much longer. The four prisoners were led down to the cells, ready to be transported back to prison. Their families all went on their way, home to adjust to a different life. I walked out of there depleted but relieved, depleted because of the emotionally draining experience but relieved it was over, and relieved he hadn't gotten a longer sentence.

The entire year was my *'Annus horribilis'*

By the end of the year my tiredness and stress was evident, my body was a skeleton, and my being was a shattered mess. I hadn't left my children's side all year, but I eventually went out for a drink. I needed it, but it wasn't me who realised that. It was a friend, a friend who was one of the few people who had been there for me when everyone else had disappeared. The friendships I had had before this terrible year are irrelevant to my life now, and time has shown me they were seasonal friendships, not real ones.

My beautiful Irish Raver, Christine.
"Come on Jen, it'll do you good. Some of the other girls are going and we'll have a laugh. You need it!" Christine pleaded.
"I don't know Chris" I tried to excuse myself from going.
"You're coming if I have to drag you, ok! Nothing else to say Jenny!" Demanded my friend.
At first I didn't want to go, I felt I didn't have it in me to go out drinking and dancing. I soon accepted how much I did need to blow off steam. My friends and I went into town, visited far too many Irish bars and got exceptionally drunk, and we all danced the night away. For the first time in almost a year I put my seriously troubled life on the back burner, just

for a while. Christine was an amazing gift to me. She helped me even when she wouldn't have known she was. She was bubbly and loud, Francis and Joseph loved her. She would come into our home and make each of us smile. She was the girlfriend of JP - the psychology student friend of Jack's and Anthony's. In the darkness of that year Christine, JP and their son Dal where like a shining light to my family, they are more than friends now. They are part of my de facto family.

After that night I begun to see things differently, like a night away from the reality of the seriousness of my current situation had enabled me to remove the cloudiness that lingered over my mind. I ultimately came to the realisation that I needed to step up and prevent my family from suffering any more than it had or would. I also saw what I had allowed to take place in my life.

The cheating, the violence, the money, the drugs, the entire sorry situation! It was then I finally accepted what I had permitted myself to become.

A victim!

Just like my mum, just like Jack's mum. The victim a woman so often becomes when she follows her man down his path, instead of carving her own. The girl I had been all those years ago when I first met Jack, the girl full of dreams had forgotten those dreams and replaced them with his. So I asked myself - could I change the direction my life looked to be going in?

Chapter Six

...Yes I certainly could!

My confidence in my abilities was pretty much shattered, I had become someone I never imagined being, someone who was dependent on her man, completely. I was ashamed of myself for not addressing this before. After all, so much had already gone on between us and I should have realised this before-hand, or to be more accurate accepted this before. You often hear that 'Love is blind', well I was finally beginning to see what that truly meant. I had been blind, not only that, I had lay down and let all this happen to me. I could have walked away many times, I should have walked away, but I hadn't. Now I was stuck in this situation, I felt I couldn't leave him now. I had to stay with him now. If I left it would be as if I'd left because he went to prison, not because of anything previous. I ridiculously thought. I was still struggling to comprehend my true feelings, but on a huge level I knew our relationship had no choice but to take a back seat. This gave me the space to make something of myself, or at least try anyway.

First things first, I needed to get myself a job so my family could survive. I hadn't worked in years, and had no real qualifications; I also believed I had no skills. Why would anyone want to employ me? How could I get a job? I pondered this and came up with a plan.

I made the decision to volunteer, in order to get a decent job. I wasn't up for working in a supermarket or something equally as boring. I wanted something a little more challenging. I always liked the thought of helping disadvantaged children, giving young people something I never had, something that would have helped me as a child - someone to talk to, someone to help. So I volunteered my services to Barnardo's.
I attended a meeting with the volunteer co-ordinator; she was a warm welcoming lady who put me at ease instantly. She introduced herself to me - "Hi I'm Angela, the volunteer co-ordinator at Barnardo's".
Angela explained what they wanted from volunteers, about the children's centre, how I would be assisting the support workers within the centre and during play sessions. She gave me information about what I should expect, and the training that would be on offer to me if I chose to take it. On my first day Angela walked me into a room busy with people preparing for a fun day at the centre, all sat around a table making banners and such

things. Angela gave me some coloured card and told me they were trying to make decorations, they were after some garlands, so I began to cut up pieces of card and loop circles together. As I sat there doing these garlands a blonde woman with a pleasant smile looked at me from across the room, she walked up to me and introduced herself. "Hiya I'm Paula! What's your name?"
"Jenny!" I replied.
Paula was witty and capable, I liked her instantly, and we would turn into life-long friends. As Angela had made me feel so welcome, and after meeting Paula, I walked out of there thrilled. I got into my car and drove home, knowing I had just made a very good decision, a decision that would put me on the right track.

I worked alongside the support workers in the children's centre, and it opened my eyes to the complexity of it all. It could be emotionally testing, draining and challenging. Working with these children, some of whom had terrible families, and at the end of the session would have to go back to those families that they were in the centre to get a break from. Not all of them, some of them were there to give their families a bit of respite from the consistent challenges of having a child with ADHD or something similar.
When I put aside what information you can become privy to, the actual job of working in the centre was fantastic. I have always adored children, I love their innocence. So I relished working with them, helping them to smile when in some cases that wasn't an everyday thing.
The centre was bright and colourful, full of toys and books. It wasn't the largest room, but it had ample space to entertain these children. It had a pool table for the older children, and many wonderful murals of Peter Pan, Sleeping Beauty and such on the walls.
Some children from there will stay with me forever. One particular young boy who was just three years old at the time, he had big brown eyes and an adorable little face, even when angry. He had an elder brother and a younger one, they all attended. This young boy, who it stated was a feisty, challenging child - their words. I really felt for this young boy, he would play alone, he looked angry and sad. Something I recognised. I worked hard trying to figure him out. I'd sit on the mat next to him playing, letting him see my games, and allowing him to come to me. What I discovered was a beautiful little boy. One day out of the blue he come and sat next to me.

"Do you like cars too?" I tentatively asked him.
"Sometimes" he replied.
"What games do you like to play most then?"
"I like stories but my mummy never reads to me."
"I love stories too, what's your favourite?"
"Any... I like this one."
He handed me 'No Matter What!' the emotion creep up on me and my eyes filled with tears.
"Would you like me to read it to you?" I asked, trying to conceal my emotion.
"Yeah!"
He bounded on to my knee, book in hand, big smile on his face. So I read for him. He loved it. All he really wanted - the thing that made him act out, appear "challenging" - was some attention.
He would run to me every time he seen me at the centre, he always asked me to read for him. His mum seen me reading to him one day, she had been there to attend a meeting with her social worker.
She came over to me and said, "I wouldn't bother, he's a little bastard."
He went to jump off my knee, but I kept hold of him. If I hadn't of held on to him, I may have jumped up and hit her myself.
"He's fine here, just having a little story aren't we mate!" I said looking at him. He just looked up at me with his sweet little smile. His mum walked away. That little boy really loved a good story. My heart hurt for him. His mother was a bad, bad mother. I would drop him home after the session, and every time I felt sick having to leave him with her. I had become privy to the confidential information about his situation, his mum liked cocaine, and men. She would be found naked asleep somewhere in her home, booze, drug paraphernalia and goodness knows what strewn across the floors, her children in the midst of it all. The boys always had bruises, social services where in the middle of trying to prove where these bruises came from, she always had a story. I wanted to bring this boy home and take care of him properly. That young boy touched my heart, and I still think about him, I wonder what became of him. I just hope they managed to get enough concrete facts to remove them all from her, because if they did not...

Time went by and Barnardo's put me on lots of training courses. One of these courses was with a company from London who were trying to set up their business in Liverpool, mentoring. So the training day was just that, teaching the volunteers what mentoring meant. One thing lead to

another and the company offered me an interview for a job.
My first interview in years, I was so nervous, and my confidence was not high. As I pulled up outside, all dressed to impress in my newly bought pink shirt and navy blue pants. I looked very professional. I started to feel like I was going to be physically sick, and yet again I made another smart decision. Blag it!! Pretend I'm confident. I have been through so much in my life surely this couldn't scare me. I walked in with pretend confidence, I walked out confident. I got the job!

So I achieved what I had set out to do, I got myself a job. Now I could look after my family. This gave me the experience that I needed. I stayed with the company for eighteen months and enjoyed my working life. I met new people, made new friends, seen a side to life I had been missing. Whilst I was in this job I saved for something I had long wanted, breast implants! I had breast fed my children and this had left me with very small breasts. I had also lost a lot of weight which added to me being self-conscious, feeling like I looked flat-chested in anything I wore. I'm a woman and I want to look like a woman in my clothes, not like a boy. As a treat to myself for all I had been through and for the job I had managed to attain I paid for breast implants. Mine where not some over inflated breasts, I went to a size C. Normal, and natural for my frame. I was absolutely over the moon with them; they most definitely boosted my confidence. I bought clothes I hadn't been able to carry off before, and bras without padding. I loved my new boobs. A well-deserved treat.
Before I left that job I got another one. A better paid one. I enjoyed my newly found career, sometimes I would struggle to deal with some of the confidential information you become aware of regarding someone else's life, but I learnt as best as I could to deal with that. I did get satisfaction from assisting people in very minor to very big ways into a better more fulfilling life, in one way or another. I only helped with suggestions, words, listening and guidance, they were the ones that truly helped themselves. My confidence grew because I finally saw that I was good at something, and that I could cope on my own.

One of the hardest jobs I had was in a teenage pregnancy unit. What I found hard was seeing, children having children. The majority of them where from truly dire back grounds, were violence and child-abuse was part and parcel of their lives. They had no concept of their responsibility. The worst case was someone whom I worked hard with, in her plight to keep her unborn child after its birth. She had previously had one child removed, she convinced me she had made mistakes but she wanted to correct them. So I worked hard to liaise with social services and other agencies in securing her a place in a twenty-four-hour secure unit. This young lady had had such an awful start in life, her own mother had schizophrenia and would bring men home at night, sending them up the stairs to her young daughter. I deeply felt for her sad situation. This young lady went into labour when I was out with her and I stayed with her throughout the birth. She had no one else. She got into the twenty-four-hour secure unit, giving her the chance to stay with her new born son. After several weeks, this young girl got in a mood over her boyfriend, picked up her child and shook him. Her child was removed from her instantly. When I turned up to her court hearing the next morning the young lady was sat there texting some guy. I was ashamed of her nonchalant attitude. I wanted to scream at her "What the fuck have you done!" But I couldn't, I kept a professional head on me and did what I needed to.

My days alone as a single parent were not easy by any stretch of the imagination, Jack had become unbearable. He would ring me constantly, from the prison phone or the mobile he had stashed away in his cell. I would hear the phone ring from down stairs and dash to it, because I knew if I missed the call the next time he'd speak to me he'd have a go at me. When I would manage to get to the phone on time...
"What have you been doing? You're out of breath!!"
"That's because I ran to get the phone you fucking idiot, I've got two kids at home what do you think I'm doing? There's no milk tray man here you know!" I would retort.
He demanded to know exactly where I was, who I was with, and what I was doing all the time. At first I would stupidly pander to his demands because I felt sorry for him, locked away from the world, never knowing what was going on. We argued all the time, until I eventually told him it was over. Enough was enough.

So we separated. It was far from amicable. He would still call constantly, if not more. He'd call me names or threaten to hurt me, I could hear the desperation in his voice. He'd get his little brother to call me if I was out at night. They even called my friends trying to catch me out, like what I did was of any business of theirs. The actions of a desperate man in prison, unable to do anything about the events in a life he had once had control over. Or rather as I would discover, he was judging me by his own standards, and the standards of his fellow co-workers. Visiting woman whose men go into prison is a common thing amongst these men I discovered. I learnt something that hurt me, the realisation that I had been right about the amount of times Jack had cheated on me. All men who partake in that lifestyle cheat, all of them, no exception. Half the time it's laid out on a plate for them by shallow women who love the excitement and so called glamour they think these men bring to their lives. These shallow men love it. When they see something they want and it's unavailable they see it as a challenge, a challenge that their money or charm can overcome. Those kinds of people have no depth. Some of these men, the very thing Jack feared did come sniffing around me. Under some illusion I would be some damsel in distress needing a man to assist me, foolishly thinking I would be interested. Obviously they all have the same morals. None!!!

I never told him about these incidents, what was the point. I never went near any of them. I actually despised them low-life so-called friends. I stopped communication all together with Jack. It was the only course of action to take.

The entire situation drove me away, and it also drove me to drink. I would work all week, go out on a Saturday, and suffer on a Sunday. Not something I'm at all proud of, but the truth is the truth. There was a period of about a year - bad for me as I'm not much of a drinker. After watching my mum hit the bottle I had never been that fond of drinking. It was a dark period in my life, because I was hiding from myself, from my pain. To be honest I was living in the sense of role reversal between Jack and I, and my inflicted ego enjoyed it. He had once been the one out partying with an array of people into the early hours whilst I sat at home wondering who exactly he was out with, now it was my turn. I wanted to know if I had someone else, if I made him cry, if I played him like he had played me would the rules still be the same. Would the forgiveness card still come out to play?? Or was that only reserved for him?? Would he like sitting in his cell with paranoia swilling around his mind, thinking of another man's hands, another man's mouth all over me?? Would he like the power someone else had to fuck up his mind?? How does it feel?? Does it hurt?? I wanted it to hurt so much he thought he would rather die.

I'd missed the party scene in my teenage years, I was preoccupied with love, but I'm certain it's something most people have to do at one point in their life, be a bit wild. I did have some fun that year, but I made mistakes too - with myself, with men, with my children. I never drank around my boys, but I did put them in their Grandmothers every Saturday night. The next day I would always be incapable of anything, I would have spent the night trying to keep up with people who are free to go home to sleep after a wild night. Instead I went home and had to try and cope with the day, but I didn't cope. I would be slouched on the couch all day. Therefore, I ruined all their weekends.

Men were never brought near my children, there wasn't that many to be honest...just enough! To be fair it was only ever about sex, and in all honesty not all of it was good. Some of it was, but the occasion when some guy I took home one night took his pants down to reveal what can only be described as less than impressive, shocked me. The night was over before I give him the chance to...well you know...take his socks off! Then there was one occasion when I found a sexy man who did have the ability to please me. I was out one night, it was a warm evening and you could smell summer in the air. I was sat outside a bar chatting to my friend, but I wasn't paying attention. I was engrossed in this man making everyone he was with laugh. Just acting the clown and fooling round. I laughed to myself as I watched him, and I knew instantly I'd be taking him home for the night.

"Are you even listening Jen?" asked my friend.

"Not really, I was watching him." I said and pointed to this dark haired blue eyed man. He caught me watching him, bought a rose off the passing seller and began to make his way over to me. I just sat there gazing at him, his eyes where mesmerising, his physique was strong and his body language was full of confidence. He came over and introduced himself, he made me laugh and we chatted for a brief time. Then he took me home. As soon as we walked through the door his mouth was on mine, his hands glided down to my thighs and he picked me up, and took me to bed. He wanted a repeat of the night, but I knew it was best left to a hot memory I could recall in my old age. I was old enough to understand I would want more than a one-night stand from him, and I didn't need any added distractions to my already complicated life.

Christine and I would go out drinking. She would always get me in messy states, one's where I'd end up dancing on tables, getting kicked out of bars after we wouldn't listen to the bouncers and repeatedly get back on those tables. The Irish sure know how to party. We'd party on in the gay bars, dancing with drag queens and chatting to everyone. I'd spend hours talking to people I didn't know, laughing with people I would never meet again. If Christine wouldn't come out with me, I would go out with my other friends, friends whose only interest was partying. That's fine, each to their own and all that. I over indulged on the Vodka most nights myself. It was such a release from my serious home life, something I needed at the time.

I had become desperate for an outlet to the situation I was in, twenty-seven and alone. A family to take care of and bills to pay, all by myself, not the life I had imagined I would be living. I realised soon enough that drinking and partying every weekend wasn't for me, especially when those drunken conversations began to bore me, people spouting the same chat time after time. I remember sitting there one night, completely drunk, talking to someone and realising; I've had this conversation with you about ten times. And honestly, it was boring the first time. Also after a while I would begin to get to the point where when everyone had gone home and I was alone, I would feel lonelier than ever. There and then I knew it had to stop. I had my children and when I was partying every weekend I wasn't capable of giving my all to them, I was tired and drained and very unhappy. What I personally needed more than anything else was to be a good mum. I knew I had to get that right if I was to be comfortable with the person I was. At that point in my life, going out drinking, I wasn't comfortable with who I was. I didn't like what I saw in the mirror, I saw a sad and lonely desperate woman who looked a lot like my mum. A selfish woman who's need to forget was coming before the needs of her children.

So my Saturday night partying stopped, not altogether, but enough, I replaced it with Saturday date nights with my boys. Something I had so much more fun with than talking nonsense with a load of drunken people. Francis, Joseph and I would visit blockbusters get a couple of DVD's, some goodies and enjoy the entertainment of our date nights. I made a conscious choice to stop fighting myself and accept what my life had become. My boys entertained me so much anyway. I really didn't need to be sad with these two in my life.
We were playing 'Rock-stars' one night - Joseph was very fond of his music, he loved Rock Dj by Robbie Williams. So there we were, Francis, Joseph and I, dancing around our living room. Joseph had his little toy guitar, strumming like a true legend. Next thing he throws the guitar down picks up the chair and goes to smash it.
"What!! What are you doing?" I said as I quickly took the chair off him.

He was completely in the zone.

"It's what rock stars do mum; why did you stop me?" He scolded me, panting away.

"Babe, we're just pretending" I said, trying to remain serious, but wanting to laugh at his audaciousness. His look of disgust at me stopping him had me and Francis in hysterics.

Francis would always make me laugh too. He was one of those children who lived in his own happy world. He always wanted to play football, so I took him to join a team. The manager had put him in goal. I'm on the sidelines watching him, the ball's coming towards him and I can see he's engrossed in a balloon flying in the sky. I shout to him "Francis the ball!" He comes around from his engrossed state to hear me say 'the ball'. Next thing I know he runs out the goal, takes the ball off the other kid and starts kicking it. Only he was aiming it back towards his own goal. Everyone's shouting at him, and he thinks it's because he's about to score, which he is...only not in the right goal.

The boys and I all went over to Christine and JP's wedding in Ireland, it was a beautiful day, an amazing weekend, two of my best friends getting married. Christine wore a flowing ivory gown that suited her free spirit perfectly. She looked absolutely beautiful, and I say that even after she had Jean (JP's Mum), and I pulling thorns off a bunch of white roses she had bought, expecting us to turn them into a beautiful bouquet. Jean and I had cuts all over our fingers, we forgave her though. It was a truly Irish affair. The priest was quirky and funny, the groom's friends (including Anthony) where merrily rambunctious. It was an entire weekends worth of live music, dancing and lots of laughter. Christine had returned home the year before and I missed her, spending time with them all always brought smiles and laughter. Francis and Joseph loved it. The two of them and Dal talked to the band, who they loved. They played darts and chatted away to all the guys, lots of the men where Jack and Anthony's friends too. The boys loved the entire weekend.

There was a trip to Amsterdam too, with Paula, my brother Anthony, and our cousin. We met up with Christine, JP, my Irish counterpart Jen and a few others once we got there. We laughed all the way, even before the smoking began. Christine discovered she was pregnant just before we got there so she was tame for a change. Paula and I went off on our own adventure, like Cheech and Chong around Amsterdam. We went into a coffee shop for a brief moment and emerged a few hours later, the mushrooms stirring some crazy hallucinations in our minds. We giggled for hours about the contents of a bin, until we moved on from that and stumbled into a club. Where we behaved impeccably I'm sure. Or maybe not, we got kicked out of the VIP area we'd managed to get into. It was a funny weekend.

That was my life. I was happy with the freedom I had to choose my own direction, and I was happy that Jack's nonsense was no longer a part of my life. My friends helped me stay sane with all our shared times, mostly though it was my boys that made me happy. We made each other happy. Francis still missed his dad, but now he just counted down the Christmas' till he would be back. Joseph didn't know any different to what he had, he wanted his dad to live with him, but unlike Francis he had nothing to base that desire on.

Through those years there was no one around to help me out financially, no one came near us. Except one old guy called Peter, a guy who struggled to provide for himself but would leave Easter Eggs on my doorstep, or post fifty pounds in a card through the door at Christmas. None of those Mr.Z's or anyone else did anything to assist my family, Jack's family. Those people he was working with just busied themselves building villas, or adding to their property portfolio, or purchasing the newest car, one or the other. I learnt all about the truth of what was going on, what Jack had done, and who he had worked with. I also very quickly learnt that these people lacked any form of empathy on any matter that was not directly their own, and that they had a deviant approach to everything. I knew I didn't want any of them around me and my children, people like that are narcissistic to the core. They are so negative that I was blessed and pleased they showed no interest in my family.

Jack's mum would mind my son's any weekend I asked her to. Especially that year I spent drinking. With that she helped me, and I was and still am grateful. Jack's sister and I had a strong bond once. She had been someone who I could trust, someone who got the two sides of Jack. Her boyfriend was good to my boys too; they both adored his silly antics. Jack's sister and Francis shared a special bond, she was young when I had him, and she would come around all the time to hang out with her cute little nephew. She loved Joseph too, but by this point she had moved away to live her own life.

As for any assistance from my own family, my mum had shown she was capable of being there for me. She still did her own bitter things in life, it's what she let herself be. She never asked how I was or showed me any emotion, but she helped me be capable of going to work by looking after my children. Anthony helped where he could too. On occasion one of them would pick Joseph up from nursery and mind him till I had finished work, or collect Francis from school for me. There was one person whom I really wouldn't off been able to manage without, my beautiful friend Sandra. She had lost her husband a few years prior and had two daughters, so we understood the dilemma each of us was in. We helped each other whenever and wherever we could. Sandra and her girls Amy and Ella are also part of my de facto family. Sandra helped me, I helped her. The children grew up together. My boys and her girls would spend lots of time playing together. Joseph was like their play doll, he got dressed up or put in suitcases, and they once played doctors on him giving him chest compressions that we luckily enough caught them doing before they hurt him. We would spend Halloween together taking them trick or treating, back when Joseph would be dressed as a pumpkin and could only say 'chicken's feet' instead of trick or treat. We would take them out for days to the circus, the fair or the arcades, where Amy would moan at Francis like an old married couple because she had spent all her two pence's and Francis wouldn't share what he had left. He did succumb to Amy's wants in the end after a tirade of moaning. Sandra and I sat watching, laughing. At Christmas when our families had gone home we would share a bottle of wine whilst the children played with the chocolate fountain. We both had similar outlooks on life, just trying to do our best by our families regardless of the situation we found ourselves in. Without my mum, Anthony and Sandra I wouldn't have been able to work, and therefore couldn't have sustained a decent life for my children.

Someone else who I like to think of as my little angel was a gentleman called Stan. One morning I was feeling really under the weather, I had been suffering from flu continually for a few months, it would go and within a few weeks it would be back. One morning as I walked to drop the boys at school I bumped into my friendly neighbour.

"Are you ok Jenny, you look awful?"

"Thanks Stan!" I tried to giggle "I'm just a little unwell today"

"You get yourself home when you drop the boys off now eh!" He quietly scolded me.

"I will Stan, thanks!" When I returned home, I made myself a hot water bottle and was on my way up the stairs when someone knocked at the door, I turned back down the stairs not really wanting to answer it, when to my surprise Stan was standing there, with a bunch of flowers and a bag.

"I don't want to intrude Jenny but I've got you a few things." he said.
"Oh Stan!" I was on the verge of tears.
"Thank-you! That's so kind!"
"It's nothing, just some things to help you get better. Now go on take them in, and get well soon." I gave Stan a quick hug. He didn't want me passing my germs on to him.
"Go in now!" he demanded.
I took the bag in and when I looked in it I started to cry. In it was lozenges, flu tables, cough medicine, chocolates, hot chocolate, honey and lemons, as well as the flowers.

Stan has always remained in my heart, and our friendship grew strong after that. His constant kindness to my family was amazing. He started buying me flowers nearly every week. He would always give the boys chocolate and biscuits. He never forgot any of our birthdays either. What a man...he definitely is 'Stan the Man!'

I will always remain grateful for all of their assistance in my life. Stan more than anyone, the majority of people judged me on Jacks actions but he never. He helped me out of sheer kindness. He had no reason to do so, no obligation. He wasn't a lonely old man, he had many family members who visited him regularly. He was just a kind individual who showed me there really was goodness in the world.

So in the midst of all this - I worked and I saved! Saved for Christmas, birthdays, holidays...Saved, saved, saved!!! All I ever felt like I was doing was saving. This was what I had to do though, to give my children a life they deserved, the most important thing in my life, the very essence of my being. We all helped each other through. Francis was my solider; he was always there to help me out, he never judged me, even when I did wrong. Joseph was growing into the cleverest, funniest child I had ever come across. Together we shared happiness. Together our love for each other washed away any negativity from the outside world. We went on holidays; beautiful little cottages in Scotland that we all wished we could stay, but alas we had to come home. School and work awaited us. Malta, a place I couldn't wait to come home from... "That was not the same hotel as the one in their pictures!"

Menorca with Christine, Sandra and their children, a wonderful little holiday, full of fun and laughter! Oh and an apparent accident involving a pram and some stairs, that resulted in a huge coggy (Liverpool talk for a huge lump on your head) and an eighty-euro bill.

We had days out; the zoo, the fair, the beach, the picture's, the chocolate factory, even a scarecrow festival. Whatever I could find to entertain them, we all enjoyed our time together. All I wanted was for them to have a childhood filled with wonderful memories.

This was my life now - my boys, my job, my friends...everything else could "Go and have a shit", as some wonderful woman I once knew would say.

Chapter Seven

Jack and I had not spoken to each other in over a year. His sister had been taking the boys to visit their dad. After the constant bitterness and nastiness between us, we both knew it was best to have no communication. So we refrained from contact, not that difficult when one of you is in prison.
Time had gone by of me answering the phone and passing it straight to Francis or Joseph, and then one day when I answered Jack asked if we could talk.
"What about Jack?"
"Maybe we could just talk Jen, I'll be out soon and we need to be capable of communicating without shouting at each other, and before you say anything I know it has all been my fault" he replied. I stayed silent.
"I am sorry Jen! For everything! I've had a long time to think, and I realise the mistakes I've made..." Jack continued.
"...I want to start putting it right Jen. I want to be a part of my children's lives. I don't want to be a weekend dad. I've already missed out on so much. I want my family back!"
"Jack so much has gone on. So much horrible shit has gone on between us. You know that it's over between you and me, even if we do manage to move on from this." I said.
"I know, but I want my kids Jen, I need them. I've missed them more than you could ever imagine"

So we talked, Jack asked if I would visit him so that we could talk properly. I knew my boys would love me to take them instead of his sister. Not that they had any issue with Jack's sister, they just wanted their mummy to take them. So I chose to once again take myself to a prison, and visit Jack.

Our first visit was tentative, so much had happened since we had seen each other last. When we first caught sight of each other a smile passed between us. A smile that said we both remembered first seeing each other. That we both remembered the love we had once shared. Our second visit not so, we had both made a decision to try and put the past behind us, for our children more than anything. We always did get on before all our troubles began, I was sure if we tried we could be friends. So I visited Jack and regaled him with little snippets of information about our children, information that only Jack was truly interested in hearing. I told Jack the story of Francis engrossed in a balloon whilst he was playing football. Jack was the one that understood the beautiful nature of Francis. About Francis ' part in a play, and how amazing he was, also how at the end of that play all the children sang Amarillo, and how Joseph had bounded onto the stage to join in. I told him about Joseph learning to ride his bike, and how he shouted to me "Are you still holding me Mummy?" long after I had let go. Stories I had wanted to share with someone, but I was always aware no one else was really interested.

Francis was near nine years old now, and he was beginning to feel the excitement that his daddy would be coming home to him. Since his dad had been gone, he had counted down the years until he would return to him. So had our little four-year-old Joseph, a boy who had never really known his daddy. I had never explained anything major to them about Jack and I separating, I just said we didn't want to see each other right now. I hadn't seen the need to upset them. Now that his release was getting closer I wondered what I would tell my two boys who couldn't wait for their daddy to come home to them.
For the first time since that very *first cut* we both talked openly and honestly. He shared with me why he had cheated. That he was a young man who felt like his girlfriend didn't want him anymore. How I had pushed him out of my life when Francis was born, at least that's how he had felt. He confessed to being an ignorant stupid man for all the times he chose drugs as part of his life, be that professional or personal usage. How guilty he had felt about the violence he had brought to my life, and the shame he felt at not protecting me like he always said he would. How sorry he was for all the mistakes he had made, and how he had learnt so much from being in prison. How he had grown as a person and now all he wanted was to try and fix the wrongs he had done, and to be a good dad.
I in turn understood where he was coming from when he felt neglected from me, I knew I had been completely absorbed in Francis, but that I had been young myself. What I had been through as a child made me obsessed with the love I felt for Francis, and if he had given me time, or talked to me about it we could have fixed it. I also felt shame on myself for ever forgiving him for all the wrongs he had done to me, and that I wasn't the same young girl I had once been. Never again would I allow any man to mistreat me.
So these visits went on, and we would talk on the phone. We became friends again. I wanted to forget the past. I knew that the past had already hurt me so much, and the future was what mattered. Jack had always put me on a pedestal and it was when we had gone our separate ways, and I

had spent the year drinking every weekend that he accepted that I too was only human. I could make mistakes too. I let Jack know I had been with other men, something he knew in his heart already. I didn't go into any details, there really was no point. Listening to him talk made me realise he wasn't the miracle I thought he was once upon a time, and he realised I wasn't the saint he had wanted me to be.

About six months before he was due for release Jack asked me if we could try again, that he would spend the rest of his life righting his wrongs that he had put on his family. I saw the prospect of a normal family, one where I could share all the different aspects of my family with Jack, one where I wasn't alone anymore. I believed Jack when he said he would never again make those mistakes. That all that business was behind him, I wanted it to be true. Our family needed it to be true. So we put the past behind us, gave each other a clean slate and tried again.

Then that day came, that cold January day, five whole years since he had been taken from our family and now he was coming back. The night before the boys had been so excited. They made Jack banners, with 'Welcome Home Daddy' and drew pictures of them all together again. They both happily stuck them around our home. Running round the house with blu-tack and posters, sticking them wherever they thought he would like. Their faces glowed from the happiness in their hearts. The boys and I had bought Jack some gifts, new underwear, and toiletries. We packed it into a basket and placed it in our lounge to give to him when he got home. We all slept together in my bed on the night before his release. They had been more excited than when it was Christmas, and the only way I could calm their excitement was to let them lay in my bed talking about their daddy until we all fell asleep together.

On that morning the three of us waited in our car anxiously. Our eyes glued to these huge wooden gates. Gates that sat in the centre of twenty foot white walls that rounded at the top, walls that no one could ever climb. Someone opened the little gate that was carved within the big gate. The boys made a hasty dash out the car towards it, then realised it wasn't him. They turned back towards me with little sad faces, and we continued waiting. Then it opened again, this time they were a little hesitant in rushing towards it. They got a glimpse of him and run like lighting into his arms, they both jumped all over him. I stood there watching this scene, two boys who had longed for their daddy finally

getting what they yearned for, both of them were crying. Jack's face was full of emotion as he carried both boys over to where I waited.
"Hello" he said, putting his arm around my waist and pulling me towards him, gently planting a kiss on my lips.
"Hello yourself Jack" I replied.
We all stayed glued to the spot as we embraced as a family. Then Jack broke the silence, "Let's get out of here eh!"
Off we went, a family, together again.
In the car Francis and Joseph sat starring at Jack, not wanting to blink in case it was a dream. Two little boys whose lives had been so affected by the path their father chose.

It was strange for us all in our own individual ways. Jack was obviously feeling the strangest, not only was he back in his home, with his children and me. He was out in the freedom, capable of going to his own fridge whenever he wanted. Going out, going to the shop, doing whatever he wanted whenever he wanted to. Not having to be at the mercy of someone else. Francis and Joseph felt strange finally having him in their home, being able to talk to him and play with him at will. Me, well I felt strange for lots of reasons. I had been standing on my own two feet, the sole provider of our lifestyle. Now Jack was back. Would I need to give up my treasured independence? I wasn't sure, for now though, I was happy. I wasn't alone anymore, and the boys had their daddy back.
That first day Francis and Joseph wouldn't leave his side, they followed him everywhere. Francis kept checking on him like he would disappear if he didn't. We all went out for lunch, then out for dinner. Jack loved his food and apart from all the obvious things he had missed, food was one of the first things he wanted to experience again. Su-mai's where top of the list. So we ate together all day. It had felt amazing to not be alone anymore. Single life had its plusses, but when you are out at a restaurant, or attending any event, you never feel more single, more alone, especially if you have previously been in a long term relationship. It's in those moments at a Wedding or a Christening or any special event, that moment everyone witnesses between whomever is the main attraction of the event, and you turn to look to the person you love, the person you have shared those moments with, and your hands touch. Your eyes meet. You are connected in that way that exists between two people who share love. It was in these moments I truly missed Jack and I was extremely happy to have him to share my life with again. At heart I am really old fashioned. I had fallen in love all those years ago, as a young teenager and

I hadn't really ever wanted anyone else. I loved the thought of being with my childhood sweetheart into our old age. So togetherness felt wonderful.

Francis watched Jack doing things, little things like the way he talked to people, the way he carried himself. He loved having the dad he had missed for so long in his life, and Jack in turn loved the little sweet innocent boy who it broke his heart to be parted from all those years ago. Joseph blew Jack away with his perception of things, and for a five-year-old his knowledge on many things - 'sharp as shit isn't he!' They all made each other laugh with their same wacky sense of humour. Jack took them camping, played football, helped them with their homework. All the normal things a father does. Francis and Joseph thrived with him back in their lives. He could teach them all the things I never could - like the off side rule, how to kick the ball, how to divide any number with his intelligent technique. He taught them some boxing skills, and all other manner of things that boys love.

Jack and I spent time together as a family, but we also made time for just us. Going out for meals, or going out to special occasions together. A couple enjoying each other's company. We would take ourselves to hotels for nights of remembering we weren't just parents; it was one of those nights I think it happened. I had begun to get very tired. I would come home from work and need a little sleep. I was grumpy and lethargic, and in the night when I felt my breasts tender and sore I knew.
"I'm pregnant Jack", I informed him the next day after I had done a test.
"What, already!" Jack laughed.

The entire year was amazing, especially for the boys. I continued with my job, until my maternity leave began. I was in supported housing at this point and earning good money. Jack would do the school runs, make dinner, clean the house, and play with the boys. We had a partnership, and everyone was enjoying our new routine. We enjoyed trips camping through the summer, with entertaining nights of BBQ's and games around the camp fire. We frequently went on leisurely walks in the great outdoors. We were a complete family again.

The year came and went too quickly. On the first of December we took out our decorations, put on some Christmas songs and began to put them up. I found Joseph in the kitchen crying.
"What's wrong my son?" I asked as I picked him up cradling him in my

arms, just as Jack walked in to witness his answer.
"This is what I've always dreamed of" Joseph replied.
A boy of six, who had never known his dad to be around, he was four months old when all this had first started, he had only ever seen his dad in a prison. The sadness that Joseph had been through hit Jack hard. Jack grabbed hold of his son and told him he would never leave him again. They both cried. Then Francis, always in his own world came running in singing songs "*Rocking around the Christmas tree*..." So Jack wiped away Joseph's tears and his own and they stayed together putting up decorations.

Our first Christmas together again was magical, we ate far too much, played games and laughed so much. Three days later we all got our best ever Christmas present.

Dj! A beautiful boy, another boy!

Born under a Christmas tree, at least that's the story I would tell Dj. He was actually born in the room of the hospital, the huge Christmas tree had been right outside the window of our room, but it was a cute tale to tell. Three boys! Whilst pregnant I had hoped it was a girl, a daughter for me to share some girlie things with, but when he was here I knew I was meant to have three boys. As I sat with my new baby, engrossed as ever, Joseph came dashing into the room. Jack had brought them both to meet their new brother. They all came in, and Joseph welled up. He was completely overwhelmed by his new brother.
I stroked Joseph's face, "Do you like him then?" I asked.
"I love him!" Joseph replied.

We took Dj home, now a family of five. As we came through the doors of our home I sat down and pressed the television remote, Jack had picked Dj up from his car seat. A song came on *'Last Christmas I gave you my heart...'* (15) **Wham**
Jack was stood beside the Christmas tree crying. "I can't believe the year I have had Jen, and it's ended with such a beautiful gift." I caressed Jack's face and sang the song again, only a new version. "This Christmas I gave you my heart and the very next day you said it could stay, next year to save me from tears I'll give it to someone like Dj", it became his little song.

The five of us stayed indoors for over a week, only going out for provisions. The boys played with their new Christmas toys, and would come and check on their new little brother every time they would hear him cry. Both of them would spend time sitting with their new brother on their knees, talking to him about the football they would play when he was older. Little Dj had to spend some time in the window; he had jaundice and needed some sunlight. It was one of the best weeks all our family had ever had, all of us ecstatic with our newest addition.

Time passed on by, winter left and spring came. I was slowly coming to grips with having three children. I had raised two alone for five years, so this was pretty smooth in comparison. Jack had well and truly settled into the outside world. He continued his fatherly duties, although I had taken back the rains of running the house. I was comfortable with it that way. Jack went out and about with his friends, he never showed any signs of taking drugs, and never became violent towards me. As far as I could tell he had kept his promise. I didn't keep tabs on what he was doing, where he was going, or who he was talking to. I didn't believe anyone owns anyone, and therefore should have to report all their moves to anyone. Jack didn't give me anything to worry about.

Until...

Chapter Eight

Seemingly out of nowhere Jack got into a scuffle with a group of young men from around our area. Next thing the police are at my door, Jack is arrested and mayhem starts again. The following day Jack got bailed. These young men were from near where we lived, so he couldn't go home. He had to go to his mother's house to stay. I was stunned by the whole thing. Jack said the lads had provoked him whilst he was out with Dj in his baby carrier. He had come home, given Dj to me and gone back out to confront these lads. He had gone to attack one of them and all of them ran off, then one of them called the police. Jack was on license and there was a distinct possibility that his license would be revoked, which meant he would go back to prison. Jack and I didn't explain all this to our children, I just allowed the boys to stay with Jack at his mum's house until we could figure out what to do next.

Jack however already had ideas of his own.
"We both dislike Liverpool Jen, don't we? There are better places to bring up our children. Maybe this is just a sign we should leave here." Jack said.
"And go where Jack?" I lamented.
"Holland!"
"And do what, you going to go back to the old days?"
"No Jen I know lots of people there and they can get me work...electricians earn good money there. You know it's better than here."

So we all talked it over, Jack said he had a friend who had said he would get work for him no problem, he was a qualified electrician after-all, he could always find work. Jack promised to sort all the living arrangements, and schooling out for the boys. Some part of me felt excited about a new life, one away from the city I had begun to loathe. Liverpool has many pitfalls, and I was always concerned about my son's growing up in a place that thrives on bravado and violence. I already knew enough about Holland to understand the different mentality it has. I thought it would be good for the boys, I believed I was making the right choice. Jack was going to leave anyway, he said he wasn't going back to prison and this way we all got to stay together. The boys had spent long enough away from him, long enough wanting and needing him and little Dj was only five months old. There was no way I was going to take that away from them, this was the right thing to do. So the decision was made. Our family would stay together. In truth I was blinded by the notion that we could move away and start afresh.

We waited a few weeks for the summer holidays to begin and then our family packed our bags and left. On the way over there I had a mix of emotions, foreboding and excitement. As the plane taxied onto the run way I looked out at the vast flatness that is Holland and hoped I was making the right decision. Jack had left a few days before us and was there to greet us at the airport. I knew straight away that the line he used about working as an electrician was a lie. As we walked through to the car park towards the car he had hired I knew, I could tell. It was written all over him. I also realised I must have known this before I left, I must of but I hadn't acknowledged it.

The boys were all excited about going to see our new place, and as we pulled up in the car outside a large yellow brick apartment block, they jumped out fascinated by the pleasant tree lined street that was about to be their new home. A beautiful apartment in a wonderful part of Amsterdam, with an amazing bakery a stone's throw away. Most people live in apartments there, and ours was a very modern Dutch apartment, all Ikea furnishings and plants everywhere. It backed onto a canal, which was our view out the veranda in the living room. Luscious trees hanging over the canal, little ducks swimming by, it was very picturesque. The front of the building was along a street full of chic looking shops; a clothes shop with its array of bright coloured garments hanging stylishly in the window, a shop with its display of elegant structured lingerie, and another one selling old fashioned wooden Dutch toys. There was an Egyptian Restaurant and a Steakhouse Restaurant, in the middle of the road on a grass verge sat a white wooden stall, with a small sitting area facing it, selling the best Thai fishcakes I ever tasted, and of course the fabulously smelling bakery. Around the corner was a playground, one of many. A short journey on foot took us to the most amazing parks a family could wish for. One had an outdoor pool in it, styled like an old Roman bath house, with its white pillars and white stone benches. Another had wild chickens darting about in the wooded area, train rides and crazy golf. The first few weeks were blissful, the ideology that we could have a new start taking over any other thoughts. No one knew us. No one knew what had gone on in our lives. Outside of the city centre most people know about Amsterdam, it is very different. It is actually rather beautiful. It is very green, and very modern. There are wonderful places to walk and play, the area around our home was full of little play areas for our children. The children there were different from the kids in Liverpool. Francis and Joseph would go into the playground and if they had a ball the older children would ask them to play football. They just played with them, no nonsense just kids playing football. The kids in the area were different, respectful and polite. They even put their litter in the bins provided. I was impressed with them. People around us appeared friendly, elegant and charismatic. A world away from the Liverpool I knew. That summer we spent lovely long days in parks, whilst the children played, having picnics and eating ice-creams. Over that summer we enjoyed our family of five, enjoyed something we all had gone without for too long. We had endless laughs about our little Dj who had taken to arguing with our dog Betty, over her biscuits. I would put food down for Betty and Dj would crawl over to her bowl and try to eat them. Betty would growl at him and he would growl back. I had to stand over Betty's bowl whilst she ate. Dj began to find his way into the cupboard were the food was kept, I'd look round for him and when I couldn't find him I would open the cupboard door and there would be my little guy in his white baby-grow, with his cute chubby little face and big brown eyes looking nonplussed at me, munching on dog biscuits. We had to tie the cupboards shut in the end, funny little man. Our time together over this summer was happy, and carefree.

After the summer holidays had ended and we had settled in to our new surroundings, the boys begun the term in their new school. Almost immediately after that, things changed. Rapidly! I didn't know anyone around the area, and Jack kept disappearing on long drawn out journeys. He said he was looking for work, he said that we needed to earn money to survive. When he was home an array of different people would come around, people who I could tell where dangerous, serious criminals, criminals on a very different scale to those back in Liverpool. All sophisticated tall svelte Dutch men with names like Diederik and Hannes. They talked to me like I was a part of their existence, never about their business, these men would never speak to a woman about their business, but in a manner that said this is us, and this is our lifestyle. This is your lifestyle. Laughing about how such and such had spent ten years in a Thai prison for murder, but now he's home and back to work...oh and he still loves those Thai girls. I got introduced to some women called Stella and Wendy, who had lived there for years. Women from Liverpool who Jack thought I would get on with, sadly though they were not my type of people. Endlessly talking about clothes and nails, it was pretentious and boring. A woman from Spain called Margarita, a very beautiful, confident lady who had her own career but loved the appeal of a criminal man. I couldn't get on with her either. She was near forty, had no children and lived completely on her own terms. I liked her confident nature but we had nothing in common. My son's got took out to huge boxing events, and to my dismay took on a Harley Davidson owned by a guy whose name I will never repeat. Only thing I will say is I heard who he was involved with and that was more than enough information. This guy's son would come around and Jack would go out onto the veranda whilst he relayed messages from his dad. I knew I had made a huge mistake. I felt trapped, and it was my own fault. I had stupidly allowed Jack to take us away from our home, naively believed this could work out in our favour. I had also not wanted to split up our family unit once again. My boys had adored having Jack back in their lives. If I stayed with him whilst he was illegal and criminal then what message was I sending to my three children, that this was the kind of life that was alright for them, because it by far was not! I didn't agree with a life of criminality and by staying I was implying that it was alright by me. If I stayed with him he could also potentially bring danger to my family, again.

Our relationship deteriorated as rapidly as my bliss. We argued relentlessly as I watched the narcissistic him return to our lives. He wished I could just accept what he did like all his friend's wives and girlfriends did. I shouted at him that I would never be what someone else wanted me to be, and if he didn't like that he could fuck off!! He became distant and cold, not even talking to me when he bothered to show his face in our home. He was beyond strange, he was far away from me, even when we lay in the same bed. Something was lost in him, some pressure I couldn't understand. I was trapped, again! Why was I so stupid? What was the reason I let this man take me in and pull me apart time after time? My relationship with him began a long time ago with such timely love. Yet for more years than was necessary I let him confuse me, I let myself be confused. It was time to break free. I couldn't take a life filled with his drama anymore, I needed peace in my life. Peace in my families lives. I knew what I was going to have to do, but I was scared, scared to be alone, again. Scared to remove my children's father from them, again, and this time it would be because that's what I had chosen. Would my children understand? Would they hate me? I didn't want to cause them any pain. So it took longer than it should to take that step. I had always just wanted to protect my children, and I knew I must protect them, even if it meant hurting them first. We had already spent a year away from everyone we knew, living a life of secrets and lies. I was living a sad and isolated life in this environment, one away from my friends and family, and I missed them all. I missed the life I had given myself when he was in prison, one that did not involve any of these one dimensional individuals. I would have to leave Jack, go home and start again.

When I told Jack enough was enough and we were going home, he appeared relieved. He didn't ask me to stay, or imply that he would come with us. He asked me to come on holiday with him for a few weeks and we could talk about our future. So we went to Spain. We stayed in a little villa with a pool. We played by the pool all day, and at night we would go down to the beach for a walk. We all had fun playing in the water, the boys running around with their blue and yellow buckets throwing it over each other, Jack like the biggest kid, soaking them all. As I sat watching this scene, taking pictures, Jack ran towards me, scooped me up in his arms and threw me in the sea. I screamed, he laughed, and the boys egged him on. We all enjoyed some family time. It was the first time we had laughed together in almost a year, in fact that was how I knew it was over between us. The laughter had stopped completely.

Jack and I both knew what was going to happen at the end of this holiday...it was the elephant in the room and we were both afraid to address it. The night before our holiday was over the elephant entered. He told me his plans, he was going to go and work for someone he knew. Someone who lived southwest and it was better for us to leave. He said he would send us money and would meet up soon.

I was stunned at his nonchalant attitude to what he was saying to me. He was cold and impassive, I screamed at him for his selfishness. I told him I would rather be poor than live a life like the one he was talking about.

"How fucking dare you leave this family after you went away from us for five years you selfish bastard!!...and do tell me Jack what happens if you get killed?"
"If I die I die! I'd like a long lie down..." his dark humour didn't go down well. I turned to give him an icy glare, putting a hole in his attempt at defrosting this argument.
"...my dad, my mum, my family will look after you!"
"What like they did when you went to prison? Because no one looked

after us then and no one's going to look after us now! We're not their responsibility Jack! This is our family, our responsibility."
We argued about it all night, but I knew he wasn't going to come home. I also knew when I looked in his eyes it was over, and not just for him and me, but for his family. The way he looked at his son's, the pain and sorrow etched in his face as he watched them play that last day. He knew he was going to leave us. He knew he was leaving his children.

Like my mother never being capable of letting her children be enough for her. Now his wasn't enough for him. I hated him. I hated how selfish the unchangeable decision *he* chose to make would impact on my beautiful son's. I had to accept the fact that I wasn't enough for him, his love for me wasn't enough for his life, for him. Why should my children have to endure that too!

I solemnly gathered our belongings, and told my children that we would be going back to Liverpool to stay, without their dad. The children were devastated that this was happening, they cried so much. Even this didn't make Jack want to save his family. Jack didn't put up any fight to keep us. This made me angrier, how could he just let us all go if he had suffered so much without us whilst he was in prison. I began to doubt every word that had ever come out of his mouth. I began to wonder if he had planned all this, even the altercation with the young lad, just so he could come over here. I could see something in his eyes, ideas of what he was going to do, plans for *his* future, selfish thoughts about his needs, his ego taking over the love and responsibility for his family. Nothing to do with the pain he was yet again inflicting on our family. He promised the children he would stay in touch, and he made false promises to see them again soon.

I woke the morning after with a sense of trepidation in the pit of my stomach. I knew what the day ahead would bring, sadness and pain. My eyes opened and I became aware that I was alone in the room. My awareness began to focus on some noise in the distance; it was a conversation between Jack and Dj.
"...puffs daddy...puffs daddy...want puffs..."
"Come here you..." I heard the sound of my child being scooped into the arms of his dad, and the planting of kisses on his chubby chops.
"Puffs daddy!!" Dj demanded.
"Ok, ok, I know you're hungry. Daddy will get you some sugar puffs." Jack giggled then abruptly stopped. I imagined the emotion crawling up from

deep inside him, in a moment of recognition. 'When will he hear his son say daddy again?'

We all picked at breakfast in silence, except for Dj, he was running around with sugar puffs sporadically scattered in his hair and clothes. We finally got ourselves together and walked towards the door, where are suitcases waited to be put in the car. Jack, Francis and Joseph gathered all our things whilst I got Dj ready. Francis sat next to his dad in the front, Dj in his baby chair in the middle of Joseph and me on the back seat. I could see Francis taking long, sad glances towards his dad as we drove in silence. As I sat in the car on the way to the airport I looked out the window at the passing ocean swishing about nonchalantly and the tears rolled from my eyes. I struggled to imagine how my life would feel, how I would feel, to live my life without him. A life without ever waking up next to him again. Not to see his face, his smile, his eyes. Not to feel his touch, smell his smell, feel his skin on mine. Not to laugh with him, or turn to him. He had been that other part of me for so long, good or bad. Now I couldn't live in his life anymore. Once I had loved with every part of me the beautiful man from all those years ago. I had no choice but to finally accept...he no longer was that man. He had gone a long time ago, and I *had* to accept that. What my children were about to go through I wasn't sure I could accept. After the arguing from the night before Jack and I had no words for each other, I was lost in the sadness my children were about to feel.

We arrived at the airport and parked the car; we filled our trolley with suitcases and began to walk towards the arrivals. Every moment, every step was like a slow moving heart retching movie. Walking towards the turning glass doors I stopped as the wind gently washed over me and I breathed in the warm atmosphere of the sunny climate, a long deep breath. This was about to get real when they had to say goodbye to him.

Francis walked tucked right in beside me, he kept looking at me for reassurance.
"It'll be alright son." I said and I held him tight next to me.
Joseph was holding on to his dad's arm as we continued towards the check-in.
"Are you all travelling?" asked the stewardess.
The boys looked at Jack, to check he was serious about not coming home with us.
"Everyone but me" Jack said in an almost inaudible voice. He distracted

himself by taking Dj out of his pram, Dj happily obliging his daddy to a cuddle. Then we made our way to passport control, our final point before we went our separate ways. The boys looked agitated and unsure.

When we got to the gate he had to say goodbye. The boys held their dad for dear life. He embraced them all, and they cried uncontrollably, wanting their daddy to stay with them, they knew what it was going to feel like to miss him. Dj yelped within the tight grasp of his daddy and his brothers, so they eventually parted. Dj played with his dad's ear whilst he stroked his face and kissed him goodbye. He put him back into his pram and gave him his teddy to keep him happy. As Jack kissed his face Dj stroked the tears off his cheek and smiled. Jack struggled to contain his emotions. He grabbed hold of Francis and Joseph, and they held each other close for a long time.
"Please come home with us dad...please!" Joseph pleaded in between heavy sobs.
" Dad has to go away to work, but I'll see you soon son I promise."
Both boys had sadness tearing through them, everyone was crying.
I turned to look at Jack that final time and he pulled me tight towards him with tears rolling down his face and whispered in my ear "I'm sorry Jen, I am!" As I looked in his eyes before I walked away from him, my heart told me I would never see him again.
"Goodbye Jack!" Tears fell endlessly, tumbling uncontrollably, tears I couldn't stop. I held Francis and Joseph close to me and told them we had to go. They watched their daddy walk away from them, and their pain was something no words could ever describe. I held them close to me, stroking their beautiful innocent faces, trying to stop their tears and repeatedly told them it will be alright. We walked through passport control and they couldn't take their eyes off their dad as he disappeared into the swarm of people. I do not know how he did that, how he walked away from his son's. How he watched their pain, rejected and abandoned them. He just walked away into the crowds, leaving a family, his family behind.

As we got through passport control and I pulled them both to the side, hugging them tight. I wiped away my tears and theirs and asked them to be strong for me, stroking their faces gently I looked deep into their eyes and promised them I would make everything alright.

Chapter Nine

When I got off that plane, laden down with suitcases and bags, holding onto Joseph's hand, whilst Francis pushed Dj in his pram, I felt absolutely numb. I was completely void of emotion. I walked through that busy airport amongst hundreds of people, with my children by my side, and felt more alone than I ever had. We all got into a taxi, and went straight to our house. Anthony had been renting it from us so luckily enough I had a home to go back to.

I knew that I no longer loved the Jack that had just let go of his family. The devastating effects of what he had just done, pouring scorn on the fact I believed him when he told me he would spend his life fixing the wrongs he had done to our family. I accept I will always love the boy I fell in love with, but he was no longer that boy, just like I was no longer that girl. My love for him was over. I couldn't understand how *he* had let his family go more than I couldn't understand anything else. After all the years he had spent in prison away from his family, his children. After us starting again and having a new baby. I just couldn't get my head around what had just happened, and I couldn't understand how he had just done what he had done. He let us go. I couldn't believe I was back in this position again. This time with three children, and this time he was completely out of our lives. I listened to a song from my yester-years, a song that spoke to me about how I had felt.

'I'd rather live in his world, than live without him in mine' (16) **Gladys Knight.**

What I couldn't comprehend now was why Jack would not have rather lived in our world instead of living without us in his.

I began all the things I needed to do. I sorted our house, and enrolled the children back into school. I was trying to get on with my life. Before I knew it several months had gone by. One day as I was sat on the settee I realised that I had been taking the boys to school, coming home putting the television on and just sitting there, staring into thin air, lost in another world, a dark, lonely world. I was depressed, worryingly depressed. I had been through so much in my life, and there had many occasions when I had felt down, I had been heartbroken, but I had always managed to snap myself out of it and carry on. This was different. I hadn't even realised what had been happening. I hadn't even realised I hadn't showered, hadn't eaten, cleaned up, walked my dog, more importantly played with my young son. The realisation scared me. Completely scared me! I knew I needed help, but I had no idea where to look for that help. I knew I needed to confide in someone, but who? I was afraid to say it out loud. I was afraid if I said it, it would make it even worse. I was afraid my children would find out that I had a black cloud suffocating me, one that had me feeling at fault for everything. I believed everything that happened was karma for going back to Jack, for going with him to Holland. For fooling myself that he had removed all the dark qualities he had gained on his life's journey, for allowing him to pour more inflictions onto my children's souls, onto my soul. I hated myself. I hated how foolish I had been. How weak I had been. How stupid I had been. This dark negative enduring suffering was my penance for my pathetic effort in life. For the sake of my children I needed to find a way to alleviate this. They deserved better than having a mother who was so drenched in pain that everything else was clouded. They already had so much to deal with. Their father had caused them inconceivable pain. They didn't need a mother that was depressed. They needed me to be strong. I knew I had to pull myself together, I just didn't know how.

I made a pact with myself, no more sitting there lost in a dark world. After I dropped my children off at school the following day, I came home put my dog on a lead, Dj in his pram and went out for a walk. I continued with this for the next few days, I struggled though as my energy was depleted. I tried talking to my friends, but my heart was too injured to converse with anyone. I kept trying, it was long and painful. I wanted to crawl into a ball and never move. To be completely honest I was having thoughts that there was no point in my life. I never contemplated suicide. I would never hurt my children like that. But my life felt pointless. I felt like I had forgotten how to smile, how to laugh, how to be happy. I felt like I would never feel those things again because I didn't deserve to feel those things. I blamed myself for this newest infliction put on my family. I followed him to Holland. I took our children there, I brought our children back. It was my fault my three beautiful children were sad. My fault they were suffering once again and missing their dad. So I carried on walking day after day, trying to blow away the pain deep in my soul.

After a while I took myself into the town centre, thinking a bit of shopping would brighten my spirits. I ventured into a book store, one of my true pleasures, although I hadn't read in over a year. I was wondering aimlessly through the aisles, not really paying as much attention as I usually would.

As I was walking towards the doors to go out I felt like something was staring at me. I had an intuitive feeling, so I turned, and I hear a voice I hadn't heard in years. The familiar voice in my head I once heard as a child, the same feeling I had in the daffodil field, and all those times after. Now it was shouting my name from the direction of a book sat idly on the shelf. My eyes squinted as I walked closer to it, as I got nearer I recognised its title as a book people had been talking about. There was just one copy left on the shelf, I picked it up, glanced at its brown exterior and red writing. Slowly glided my fingers over the title, and instantly felt some sense of comfort. I bought the book and left the store. 'The Secret'.

This was the point my life went in an entirely new direction. It wasn't essentially the book, more the message I received, loud and clear, the message that I had so desperately needed to receive. The help that was so necessary at a point in my life when I did not know how to pull myself out of depression.

That message was to appreciate all the things I already had in my life, for the things I had were more important to me than that what I had lost. I had my children, the greatest loves of my life. The biggest blessing that was ever bestowed on me had been my children. What more could I possibly ever need in my life, what could be more important than the three amazing children I had to walk my journey through life with. Nothing! I collected my boys from school with a big smile on my face, the first they had seen from me in too long. That night over dinner I chatted to my children, and laughed with them. I felt a glimmer of light peeking through the darkness. I knew that there was something very real to my life, there definitely was a point to life, and it was sitting at the table with me. The boys were all in good form, and appeared to be thriving off their mum's new found positive energy. They all, in turn, amused me, and each other. I enjoyed the sound of laughter, something I had forgotten to do. The book also taught me the power of positive thought. This changed who I was. It made me aware of how negative I had been. How I had allowed myself to be sucked into a life built on inflictions from my past, and from the words of other people. This did not make me unhappy, rather the opposite. I understood how my life had gone in the directions it had. Now *I* was going to take *my* life in my own hands and steer it in a new direction. So I had taken the first steps in pulling myself from the depths of despair. I had been strong before, I had raised my family alone before. I could do it again.

It wasn't an easy journey, and it certainly did not happen overnight. Dark versus light! It was a journey of strength and will power. At first I used a technique that had assisted me on my journey before. I pretended. I tricked my mind with affirmations. "I'm happy, I'm capable!" I repeated this affirmation to myself ridiculous amounts of times and then the light from my heart began diminishing the darkness in my mind. I knew that the mind could not distinguish the difference between imagination and reality, the mind only knows what you tell it. So I plodded on day after day, one small step at a time, raising the bar on my positivity daily. I had always been a positive individual through my life, I always found something positive from a bad situation, and I told myself - sitting on the dark side was not for me. To progress I knew I would need to change my thoughts, my words, my actions. I began to understand the journey of my life. It had not always been as simple as I had expected it to be, it had not always been as simple as I wanted it to be. I did not know the things that awaited me around those corners, I only saw how blind I had been once I had turned smack bang into those corners. Sometimes the corners I turned had shocked, hurt and destroyed me. Making me forget all that I had known before, making me forget the person I once was. Sometimes they surprised, amazed and delighted me, still changing me from the person I had been. I needed to free myself of the negative qualities I had and this new corner I had turned was the beginning of a profound transformation.

One thing that was definite in my mind was that everything about that life - Jack's bizarre world - everyone within that life had to be removed from my family's future. My children were never going to follow the path Jack had taken, never! They would not be witnesses of that criminal, egotistical, selfish life as something to aspire to. To be fair it wasn't hard to remove them, it's a funny world...'money'. When you have it people are all too interested in you and your life, but when it goes so do the fickle. So I never went or allowed my children to have anything to do with any of them. Jack's mum and sister where different, and the boy's still seen Jack's little brother but that was because he still lived at home with his mum. As for me I never belonged in that world, it had never felt right, like a square peg in a round hole. So to be completely free of it was a blessing.

I began applying for jobs, knowing I would find something. I used the power of positive thought. I knew this meant that Dj would need to go into childcare, but my family needed me to work, I needed to work, if only to assist in alleviating my troubled mind. Well that and the need to provide for my family. I decided a break would do us all good, so we booked a little trip to see the beautiful Christine in Ireland. The holiday was lovely, the boys thoroughly enjoyed it. JP took them out on little adventures, to look at haunted houses, and ghost estates that had been started but not finished due to the financial crisis Ireland was in the midst of. Whilst Dj played in their garden, Christine and I sat chatting. As is always present in the emerald Isle, a party was on. I had a few drinks and joined in, although I could see in myself I had lost my mojo, but this was something I was working on, so I just enjoyed what I could about the moment. I felt better than I had since everything that had gone on in Holland.

On our return home, I opened my mail and to my surprise I had acquired three job interviews. One of them was an hour after we had returned. I showered and dressed quickly. I had to leave the boys in the car whilst I attended the interview, giving Francis strict instructions to behave and watch his brothers. Francis was now twelve and Joseph was eight, we worked as a team and they entertained Dj whilst I was gone. Over the next few days I attended the other two interviews. I was good at appearing confident, I had done it before. I passed the interview on all three, and was offered jobs on all. I was elated. I chose one that struck a chord for it had Francis' name in its title. So I had done it again, I had a new job to go to, and new beginnings.

I read a lot and tried to enjoy everything I had in life, another book coincidentally came my way. I had over-heard someone talking about it the day before. So when I was in a charity shop looking through the books and I look and see this book just there sitting on top of some others. I wasn't sure what it was about but I had a good feeling about it. I picked it up and bought it, the best thirty pence I have ever spent. This book taught me things I hadn't realised about life. It taught me about energy, about everyone's energy, and how that energy can be affected by the words of other people, how people behave in certain ways, due to inflictions from their past. The Celestine Prophecy! Without doubt in my top best books I have ever read. It helped me evolve as a person, another positive step on my journey.

After reading this book I became aware of myself like never before. I began to study myself and change the things I didn't like, or the aspects about me that did not serve me any longer in my journey to be the person I wanted to be. My first step was to address every part of myself, good or bad. So I bought myself a small note book and made two columns, the headings of these columns was 'Good' & 'Changeable'. Underneath both I listed all the things I liked about myself, and all the things I would like to change. It wasn't called good & bad because I had accepted at heart I was a decent person, and therefore nothing about me was bad. I was just in need of some readjusting, and I liked the word changeable. I liked that it meant things I 'could' change. So the good things listed like this; a loving mum, good homemaker, liked to have a laugh, cared about people, was capable, efficient and trustworthy, strong, bold (although could be bolder), did not suffer fools (except by the name of Jack, but no longer) etc... The changeables listed like this; impatience, hot headed, fear of failure, stubborn, not always having the ability to see other people's point of view, had - for far too long - allowed other people's choices to affect my life (my parents and Jack), could be distant and unapproachable, in times of stress became introverted and irritable, could pay more attention to the smaller things in life.

I began to see those good points and be proud of them. I hadn't had a good childhood, and continuing that cycle is easier than breaking it. For me though breaking it was the only choice. As soon as Francis came into the world I broke that cycle. No mind games, no ego's, no fear of my child, I just loved him. I showered him with affection and love, praised all his many achievements. I let him know how special he was, and how he could achieve anything in his life through hard work and determination. Encouraged him to be true to the person he was, no matter what other people thought. I had taken this stance with all my children. The individual amazing people they are is testament to the cycle I had rightly broken. Jack had begun to berate my strength many years ago. He had tried to quash that by making me feel like I was wrong to believe I was strong. When we would argue, he would scream at me saying "You've got balls bigger than any man, haven't you!" Something he had loved about me in the early days, further down the line this had changed. The dynamics of our relationship changed, and the things he had loved about me had become the things he despised. In the heat of the moment I would say yes I was as strong as any man, in fact probably stronger. After it I always felt ashamed of my strength, thinking only men are meant to be strong. Now for the first time in far too long I accepted my strength as a valid asset to assist in my progression, as the asset that had always helped me.

A lot of things I was able to change with relative ease. I began practising meditation in order to eradicate my impatience and my hot-headedness, and to calm my stressed mind. Meditation became a blessing in my life, it assisted to calm me down, to help me focus, and relieve my deep fears and my anxieties in life. I worked on my stubborn nature - I still have to work on this one sometimes. I began to listen more to what people were saying, truly listening to them. Not listening just to reply which is how most conversations go, and to see the truth behind what people were actually saying. One changeable I needed to address was my fear of failure, what did I fear failing at? Being a good enough mum! What if my children's childhood was unhappy? Fear of failing myself, I knew I was capable of more than I had yet achieved. I had always wanted to be a writer, yet never found the time to explore it more. I was obviously afraid I wouldn't succeed. Looking at the situation in black and white allowed me to see that I knew I was a good mum, and I had tried to give everything I could to my children. Through circumstances out of my control they would have issues, they did feel pain. I had to accept that I could not do anything but support them through these things, and continue to give them all my love with hope it was enough to brighten their lives. As for writing, I needed to find some time. I imagined I would need somehow to be capable of taking a year out in order to write. That or a win on the lottery to give me that time.

I started to take more notice of how a lot of adults carried inflictions around within them that had been born from something in their childhood. Like the nasty man who lived next door to me, who shouted at his wife, his children, his dog in the same nasty venomous voice all day, every day. I had discovered one of my cousins went to school with this man, and he told me how he was a kid that was bullied. Then I understood why he was doing this, he wanted/needed to feel in control. The victim became the bully. Not an unusual story.
Jack carried inflictions caused by his nefarious father and his mother's lack of concern. Jack's father carried inflictions caused by his own alcoholic violent father. My father carried inflictions caused by unaddressed jealousy the oldest child feels when his mother's love has to be shared between eleven others, and the violence and head games that were ever present in his childhood family, added to those inflictions. My mother had

inflictions that began with the death of her mother, added by her husband and never dealt with. We all had inflictions.

I carried many around! I could be volatile; aggression would brim out of me when pushed, because it's what I learnt as a child. I could be distant and unapproachable because in the past when I had been hurt, I had retreated into myself and found comfort in trusting only in myself. I had had major trust issues that stemmed from my parent's wrongdoings and Jack betrayals. I wasn't afraid of any person, this was because my father had always scared me as a small child, and when I had gotten old enough to stick up for myself to the man I always feared then no one else was going to scare me. Not even Jack, to a certain extent, that's why our relationship had become so volatile, if I had backed down more there may have been less violence, but then he would have completely emotionally controlled me. I was also carrying the abandonment infliction. My father had abandoned me as a young child. He had never shown me any love, I never felt important to him and then he left. Jack had abandoned me, once when he first broke my heart, and then when he had turned his back on his family. I was more inflicted than I realised. Even small unimportant things like the fact I always wanted my home to be immaculate, this was due to my home as a child being rather dirty. How I always wanted to have biscuits in our cupboard for my children, because as a child we had been poor and biscuits were a rarity, all inflictions from childhood. Now it was time to deal with those afflictions and move away from them. Well some of them anyway, I've made my bed with that biscuits business in my home, my children would cause anarchy if I remove that one. In my childhood home love was never shown, it was never said. No happiness. No laughter, no togetherness. No communication, nothing but silence, or shouting, each saying no real words. No celebration. No magic at Christmas. No birthday cakes or birthday songs. But without these things I wouldn't be the mum I am. Then I realised all of my inflictions could be steered towards gaining something positive. Now that I am ready to learn and let go!

The more I analysed myself, the more insight I gained on the workings of the mind, and the reasons I had behaved in certain ways, the bigger my empathy towards other people grew. I was appreciating life in a whole new light.

Two emotions are the root of every other emotion an individual feel's, love and fear. Finally, a level of understanding the true nature of human beings seeped into me, and I began to evolve as a person. I understood the fear of rejection, of failure, of ridicule. The fear of believing in yourself! Now I understood this, now I could change the way I viewed life, and then life begun to change.

'Our deepest fear is not that we are inadequate. Our deepest fear is that we are powerful beyond measure. It is our light not our darkness that frightens us.'

Only it's not easy to be in the midst of any given situation, and accept there is a lesson to be learnt. You need to be truly enlightened to be in a difficult situation and see that there is a reason for the experience. And I most certainly wasn't enlightened. Not yet anyway....

Chapter Ten

There on the mat at the foot of my front door lay a brown envelope addressed to Jack. Strangely we had not received any post for Jack since our return. I do believe the police had a hand in that, they had wanted to find Jack, and would do so at any cost. They had come to my house many times looking for him. We even had a van load of them bursting through my door one sunny morning as I mopped the floor. Telling me they had received a call from someone saying they had heard a women screaming for 'help', and as there was a wanted man from this address it was their duty to protect us. Yeah, yeah!! I'm sure these people think I am stupid. It's funny how when they try to come into your home for a look around and you won't let them without a warrant, that this happens. They don't need a warrant to come into your home if there has been a call of this nature. Apparently it is illegal to intercept Royal Mail, though I am aware this has never prevented them before. It was a strange occurrence that no mail had been delivered for him until this letter. As I opened it I was not prepared for the information it contained. The letter was from the Land Registry; it was regarding our home. Turns out Jack had used several credit cards to fund his existence, and now, as they had not had any payments or had any response to the multiple letters they had apparently already sent, the action taken was a Court Order to repossess our house.

My heart sank. How could this happen? We had been home for nearly two years and not one letter had come for Jack in that time. How could Jack do this to us, he had already neglected every responsibility a parent has to their family. Now he had underhandedly, nefariously racked up bills that he had no intention of paying. Capitalizing on our degradation, sending us to rack and ruin. The tears streamed down my face. Was this for real? I felt the urge to vomit, and ran up the stairs to the toilet. Where I stayed for I don't know how long, completely shell shocked. How after all my positive thinking, all my work to regain, and retain some happiness was this happening. I sat at the top of my stairs, the place I had sat many times, always after I had received some bad news and needed to digest what was happening. For a while I sat there in shock at the devastating situation that was about to happen to my family. As the shock lapsed and the reality seeped in, I took action. I contacted a solicitor for some advice. I also contacted the Land Registry, they however "would only speak to Mr. Jones", but Mr. Jones had been missing for some time. They were uninterested in my plight.

Two days later I entered the office of a solicitor who dealt in family law. The solicitor guided me into a small room at the side of the reception, pointed towards a seat and suggested I sit down. This dark haired man in a grey expensively cut suit looked upon me and requested I explain the situation to him. So I began; how Jack was missing, how we had no contact from him in over two years. How he had been to prison for five years, a year or so after his release he went missing, how he was wanted by the police, and that they could check this on their records. Then I showed the solicitor the letter, and asked for his advice. This was a complex matter he informed me, for one it is of a criminal nature, due to Jack revoking the terms of his license. Then it was a family matter, and then as for the house it was commercial law. All this made it far too complicated for just one solicitor to deal with, I may have to seek the assistance of other solicitors. After some information sharing on my income, it turns out I earned slightly over the limit to apply for legal aid. "So this consultation is free, but to continue you will need to put down five hundred pounds, and then the cost of every letter, every phone call, and any court hearings attended would be added to that. Therefore, unless you have that money we cannot help you, sorry." That was the gist of the conversation.

Day after day I tried to come up with how I could fix this. Could I pay off the credit card bills? No! It was too late for that. Could I register Jack missing or dead and put the house in the boys' name until they turned eighteen. No, not possible! Jack would need to be missing for seven years before you could take that measure. Could I get a mortgage and buy the house? No, I didn't earn enough to do that. Then what!!! What was I going to do? I couldn't see a way out, and the weight on my shoulders was becoming heavier, and heavier. My mind was in turmoil. My positive approach took a huge step back. How could I fix this? This was our home, it was the only thing we had, the only security Jack left us with, and now he had heinously taken that away from us too. I tried to contact Jack through one of his family. Two weeks later Jack made a very brief call to us, and his only answer to me was "I can't do anything to help". He sounded erratic and unconcerned. He spoke to our children for the first time in far too long, he promised them he had his plane ticket booked and would be back with them soon, and he would make it up to them for the time he had been away. The entire thing lasted just a merge few minutes. I told my children "perhaps daddy's got it wrong", as I held them whilst they cried for him, yet again. Whilst I wanted to say "Your dad's a bastard, who has turned his back on his responsibility to this family". Joseph didn't believe his daddy had got it wrong and went to sit by the window day after day waiting for his dad to return. Poor little Joseph, a young boy who had adored finally having his dad back in his life once before, was now desperate to have him back again. A boy who loved how he could challenge his dad's mind and amuse him with his sarcastic sense of humour. A boy who had been perpetually missing his dad since he was a tiny child, a boy who believed him when he said he was on his way home. This affected Joseph beyond words. I was left to pick up the pieces from the complete lies he had told his children, he had no plane tickets booked nor did he intend to come home. I was also left to find an answer to our impending problem by myself.

The burden was immense; I was scared, stressed, and anxious beyond imagination. Night after night I would lay awake. Insomnia killing my soul! I'd toss and turn all night, my mind wouldn't shut down, every detail of the situation would be rolling around in my head. I tried taking sleeping tablets but they didn't work. I tried to down a shot of whisky, but this only resulted in me throwing up in my kitchen sink. I tried everything, but sleep wouldn't come. After nearly two weeks of no sleep I just lay there crying just wanting to forget my problem for one night, just one night so I could sleep. Sleep deprivation can do strange things to a person. Some days I wasn't thinking about my house, or my life, or my children. I had endless songs playing over, and over in my mind. Sometimes just one line from a song on repeat, it wouldn't go away. It wouldn't stop! *'I'd be smiling if I wasn't so desperate...' '...I'd be patient if I had the time...be patient if I had the time...patient if I had the time...patient...if I had the time' '...soon as I find out how to move from the back of the line...move form the back of the line...back of the line...back of the line...'* (17) **Emilie Sande.**

I stood on the precipice between sanity and madness. Some days I didn't know which I was, at times I wanted to scream at myself, or hit my head on the floor in order to stop the songs playing perpetually around and around in my fucked up mind. I could not comprehend. I could not concentrate, could not talk or think. I needed to sleep. No answer would come to me whilst I was bordering on the insane. One night I picked up the IPad and tried something different. Sleep hypnosis. IPad ready! Earphones on! YouTube valiantly to the rescue! I fell into a deep, deep sleep, a wonderful much needed sleep. When I awoke I had no thoughts. I just felt drowsy with a slight sense of peace. The next night I did the same, and the night after. Until I felt myself again, back to sanity. The songs in my head stopped, and an answer came. The only answer there was.

Move out!

In celebration of an answer I went to sing a little tune to myself, then my mind shouted 'how's about you fuck off for a bit, just for a while!' I couldn't listen to another song. So I did a little jig in the middle of my bedroom instead.

I knew I had every right to fight for what belonged to me, and my children. I had paid the mortgage on our home since Jack had gone to prison. My name wasn't on the mortgage because I wasn't working when we bought the house due to my broken ankle all those years ago. I knew I should have changed that, made sure my name was put on the mortgage, but I never did. Now it was too late. I didn't want to fight for it, some people thought I was mad to walk away from tens of thousands of pounds but I didn't see money being something to cause me this amount of stress. I was trying to be happy, trying to move on from my past. I knew if I fought for my house, my money, the stress would damage me. Money was not that important to me, my family was struggling financially but my sanity and happiness was imperative.

I took my boys out for dinner, we sat around the table chatting away, making each other laugh or annoying each other. Dj pulled Francis's hair, whilst Francis teased Joseph about something, and Joseph tried to ignore Francis instead pulling funny faces at Dj. There was food all over Dj and plenty on the table. I just sat watching them, smiling to myself, no matter what happened I had my three boys, their madness amused me. These three innocent boys had no clue what had gone on, no idea that their dad they so desperately wanted was causing our family so much devastation. No understanding that not only had he never sent us a penny since he left, now he had used our home as collateral to fund whatever was going on in his life. To the point of us losing it! How could they understand, I didn't want them to know. They had enough to deal with knowing he did not contact them, feeling he had abandoned them. They didn't need extra reasons to feel sad. As we left the restaurant and jumped into our car I looked at them all and knew that this was always going to be the way it was from now on, me and my boys.

'You are my sonshine, my only sonshine! You make me happy, when skies are grey!'

Happiness enveloped me as I could see that with them I could tackle anything. I slept soundly that night.

Francis at this point was enjoying some new found freedom. For the first time in his life he was allowed to go about his business without me. He was fourteen going on fifteen and girls had become a part of his life. I can't say I was pleased for he was out every night kissing a multitude of different girls. The world for young kids now is a world away from the one I grew up in. I blame technology for the wave of promiscuity that emerges from these young kids. Francis however was not at all fazed. In-fact he loved it! What young boy wouldn't? Francis was so good looking, with his big brown eyes and extra thick long eye lashes. The kind women paid handsomely for, were his natural eye lashes, and that smile. I always knew once girls come on the scene it would end his innocence. He was still a good boy, helping around the house and playing with his brothers, but he was always in a rush so he could leave to go out. Girls awaited, and anyone who has raised young teenage boys knows that the only things on their mind are girls. It's were it starts and I've never known were it ends. Every male I know is still the same into their old age... men! It's all about their second brain, or first in some cases, which resides down south and is their main priority.

When girls were not distracting his mind Francis was suffering. The impact of his father's abandonment tearing him apart, he would be fine for months and then he would be moody for days. The end result would be when he would come home and go straight up to his room, slamming the door closed. All I would hear was the sound of fist hitting walls or wood and I would rush up the stairs. Opening his door, I would witness my beautiful son swearing and cursing the man causing his pain as he smashed up his room. I would try to grab hold of him but he was far too strong and I could not always bend him to stop. After moments of heart breaking anger would pass he would fall forlornly onto his bed and cry. The frustration of not being capable of contacting his dad and have some form of communication, anything; anger...love...hate. Something concrete to help him find some understanding. My boy had none and no way to relieve this frustration he held within, other than these outbursts of rage. I had no answers for him. I didn't know why? I didn't know if or when it would end. All I could do was let him know how much I loved him. That I would support him, and that he must never blame himself for the transgressions of his father. I worried endlessly about the effect this was having on him. I had an idea to have him learn to meditate in the hope it could calm his anger, and to my relief he went for it. What Francis got from meditation was unbelievable. I honestly believe it saved him from a destructive path. He talked to me about what happened to him whilst meditating. Francis described how whilst meditating he would go into a room, a dirty horrible room were the windows, the floors and the couch that sat in the middle of the room were filthy. On that couch sat his dad. Over time he kept seeing his dad on that couch, until he had a breakthrough moment. He went into the room, kicked his dad out, and smashed everything up in the room, including the windows. Then on his next meditation he went back into this room, only this time it was all bright and clean. With a new couch sat in the middle, when he looked at the couch his brothers and I were sat on it smiling at him. After that Francis really changed, it was as if he dealt with the dangerous level of anger he carried inside and moved on as best he could. Then Francis' life was becoming his own, one that was his own story instead of whatever his father or I had put on him, as it should be.

Joseph, my lovely beautiful Joseph was excelling at school. He is so sharp it's scary. Can't get nothing passed Joseph. He was and always will be the highlight of any dinner table we sit around. He is forever amusing people with his quick wit and sarcastic humour. He excels for a crowd too. Definitely needs to be on stage that kid, unbelievable! He makes me laugh like no other. He is so sweet and adores me so much. He always wants to look after me, offering to help me, or treating me to a whispa when he has money, the way to his mother's heart, a whispa. He too was suffering from the damage his dad had done. Only Joseph dealt with it differently. He would be quietly obstinate and sullen, going to his room by himself thinking about what his dad had done. I would have to force him to tell me how he felt. Explaining bottling it up would only hurt him more. I got him to learn to meditate too, and it helped relieve some of the stress he held inside. He felt that his dad had betrayed him because he had promised him when he came home from prison he would never leave him again, and when he had said he was on his way home to him, which he wasn't. I helped him see that this was his dad's transgression never his. Joseph is a sensitive individual and I am aware that this part of his life will have a profound effect on all he does. I'm also aware that I need to be the best mother possible to him, understanding his frustration and validating his emotions so he feels secure and hopefully not effected so deeply it negatively projects into his life.

My little Dj who can go gozzy for far too long that I become afraid I'm going to have to crack him over the head to end it. He was about to start school; he had stopped fighting with the dog over the biscuits but he was still a crazy little guy. Coming down stairs in some outfit he had put together, drawing pictures all over my walls, or jumping out at me when I would come out the bathroom. He has a very expressive face and is always pulling some freaky faces, or making freaky noises. He smiles that smile that makes every morning I see him feel like the world is good, that is until someone ruins his game and then he tears the house down. I'm certain he's the craziest cat alive. He's a lover of the nude effect. He strips off and runs around like he's been at the catnip. It's constant fun and games, oh and plenty of noise in a house with three boys. His pain would come later.

Over the next few months I threw away, and packed away our entire belongings. It was therapeutic for me to remove everything that belonged to Jack, or anything he had every given me. I gave it to charity, binned it, or sold it. Either way it went. I liked how that felt. I was beginning to see this as a blessing, the house was in Jack's name so if this hadn't of happened I would always be in *his* house. The loss of this house was unburdening me, and my problems brought opportunity. This way I was moving to a new chapter without Jack remaining in any part of it. I knew my children could not understand that, but this family needed to walk away from the enduring pain he put upon us for far too long. Our lives had been centred round him, in every way. It had been him that had caused all our dramas, all our suffering. He even managed to cause us pain when he wasn't around. Enough now, it needs to end. He needs to be removed from us. The man he had turned into didn't deserve this family anyway. I would say that I should have left him when he first cheated on me, but then I wouldn't have Joseph. If I hadn't of tried again after he came home from prison, I wouldn't have Dj. So I don't feel regret about decisions I have made, but now every part of him needs to go. We *need* to start afresh.

Chapter Eleven

One morning in the shower I noticed I had three lumps under my right breast, and I had been having pains shooting down my right arm and in my back, directly behind where I found the lumps. The thought of cancer is on everyone's mind when you feel a lump. Although I knew it was quite possibly my breast implants. I did not want to panic. I made an appointment straight away with my Doctor. "There is something there Jennifer I'm going to refer you to the breast clinic. Try not to worry, they will do a scan and this will help to see what it is". I went home to await my appointment; I didn't feel too worried. I had a gut feeling it was the implants.

Within a few days my appointment came. As I walked into the Linda McCartney wing of my local hospital, I observed all the ladies there, all with their own concern written across their faces. I knew out of the ten or so women waiting, at least one of them could get some devastating news, news that would inevitably change their entire life. All the women had been given a basket and a gown, "Take your top layers off, and put your clothes in the basket. Then take a seat in the waiting room."
So there we all sat with our gowns on, and our basket next to us. Some women looked calmer than others. Some had even brought a book to read. I just sat watching, and wondering what news I was going to come out of there with.
"Jennifer Smith" they called.
"This way" they walked me into a room.
"Lie down on the bed Jennifer, and remove your gown." They pleasantly asked me.
The nurse squeezed on some lubricant gel, same as the one they use to scan you when you're pregnant I assumed, and then they place on the ultra-sound scanner. I was trying to concentrate on anything other than what was going on. Like the coffee cup on the side, it was cream with lilac stripes and had coffee stains all down it. I was undecided if it had been there for days, it looked so grubby. I lay staring at the cup for ages, pondering its past contents. They scanned my breasts, and under both my arms. After a long time of scanning, they wiped away the gel and asked me to wait in the waiting area for the consultant.
"Your right breast implant has ruptured, the implant has dispersed and gone into the nodes beneath your right arm, we will have to operate to remove the implants, and the nodes." The consultant was straight to the

point.
"I will have you booked in within the week, my colleague will bring in some consent forms for you to sign, and I will go and get you a date. Do you have any questions?"
"No, I erm...no. I'm not sure." I stuttered.
"You will need to find out if your implants where the PIP implants Jennifer. You will need to speak to the clinic that you attended." The consultant was amazingly emphatic.
I walked out of there and breathed a heavy breath full of relief, then when I looked around me I felt guilty - 'These women where here for other issues, and here I am because of these implants' I thought. I was just so thankful it wasn't cancer. I headed home to my children. I had briefly considered what would happen to my boys if I died. I wouldn't trust anyone to raise them, no one! Thankfully that was not an issue.

My operation was booked for the following week, I informed my work, Sandra was going to take care of the boys and I set off for hospital. I was only in overnight, and then after I had to have home care until the tubes hanging out of me could be removed. They were attached to drain excess fluid. I'm sure once patients would have stayed in hospital but these days you're out as soon as possible. Sandra came to collected me, when she walked in and took a look at the state her friend was in, she went straight up to the nurse.
"She shouldn't be going home, look at her! She's got them tubes hanging out of her and she looks awful". The nurse calmly told my concerned friend that I would recover better in my own home, and that a nurse would be out every day. So Sandra helped me place the drain bags and the tubes into a plastic bag and then she tied it around me with the rope from my dressing gown to stop it swaying about causing me even more pain. Then she helped me get dressed, and took me home. I could not ever have foreseen what was about to happen to me. I had felt strange since I had woken from the operation, excessive crying and sad defeat lulling in my being, but I put that down to the anaesthetic.
When I got home Sandra helped me to undress and I climbed into my bed a quivering mess. I fell asleep and almost instantly began to dream.

I was standing on a stepping stone in the middle of a rocky river, wearing only the stripy gown I had worn during the operation. Ahead of me were more stepping stones, the one directly in front of me looked unsteady and dangerous, after that the stones and the river looked calm and peaceful, I could see the clear unspoilt land on the other side looked sunny and bright. I knew I wanted to be there, not stuck on this stone, afraid to move. None of the stones was close enough to step right onto. I turned behind me to see an eerily dark scene. I could see I was in the middle of the river, I glanced at the stones I had already crossed; they all looked rough and unsteady, with the river raging amongst them. The bank was filled with thorny bramble bushes as far along as I could see. I wondered how I had managed to get to where I was. It was as if a black cloud hung over it, and the darkness frightened me. I was more fearful than I had ever been, my heart pounded in my chest, and I was shaking uncontrollably. I swayed from side to side trying to find my balance, as the strong current of the river swashed around my bare feet, it knocked me over onto my knees. I curled up tight trying to hang onto the stone. I knew I would have to jump to the next one.

Then I woke up. My boys had come home from school and had bounded into my room to see me. I talked quietly to them, and they said they had missed me whilst I was in hospital. After a while they all went about their own thing, Sandra took Joseph and Dj to her house for dinner. Francis went out with his friends, and I was alone again. I fell back asleep.

As soon as I fell asleep I was in the same place I had been before I had woken up, on a rocky stone about to fall off. I unsteadily stumbled to my feet and leapt into the air praying to land on the next stone. As I descended from the air back down I missed, my fingertips grazed the edge of stone as I plummeted deep into the river. My body floated down until it slumped heavily onto the river bed. My eyes were open and I was aware; I could see and feel the gravel and stones beneath me, and the water all around me. I could see the sun's rays that bounced through the reeds and onto the floor, quietness surrounded me as I lay motionless at the bottom of the river bed. I knew I was still alive, yet I felt like I had died.

When I awoke I couldn't stop crying, I was confused and afraid. Then I would fall asleep again, where I would just be in my body lying on the bottom of the river bed in silence. My friends kept trying to talk to me. Sandra would come into my room and ask if I needed anything? "No!" was all I could say. She thought I just needed to sleep and would take care of Dj at her house for me. Every time Christine would call from Ireland I couldn't string together a sentence, I would just sob down the phone. Christine would ask me, "Are you ok? What's happened? Can I help?" I couldn't answer. My friends where worried about me, I had always been strong. They couldn't understand what was going on, but then neither did I. I had no words to explain what was happening to me.

My boys kept coming in to check on me, if I was awake Francis would always ask me if I needed anything. He would bring me cups of tea; he kept trying to get me to eat something. He kept tidying up for me, and playing with Dj. Dj would come in and just lay next to me. Joseph would bring me chocolate the only thing I managed to eat, he would sit on the bed next to me asking me how I was feeling. I was in some semi-comatose state and only remember fumbling with the wrapper to get to the chocolate. The majority of the time I would be asleep when they would come in, and my friends were keeping them busy. One-night Joseph came in and saw me crying and I told him it was because I felt unclean, that my hair was all greasy and I felt horrible. How could I explain what was going on in my head, I couldn't understand myself. Joseph being the loving son he is said "Come on mum I'll help you wash your hair".
So we went into the bathroom and I knelt over the bath whilst Joseph showered my hair. The water from the shower masked the tears rolling down my face at the beautiful gesture of my young boy. Joseph brushed my hair when he was done, "Do you feel better mum?" he asked, looking at me with his beautiful green eyes.
"I certainly do!" I embraced Joseph tenderly.

When I would wake I knew I had woken from the dream, but even awake I felt like I was there lying at the bottom of that river bed. I slept for days, and every time I slept I was there on the river bed, and when I was awake I was there on that river bed. As I lay there awake on my own bed, in this semi-conscious state I started to sense a different me, me but another me, standing in the corner watching myself. Sometimes I was me that was lying in my bed, a soul suffering, knowing in the corner there was another me watching. Other times I was the me in the corner watching, conscious of my suffering but not concerned, no emotion, just present, watching. It was a presence I cannot fully describe. My mind was in some three dimensional state, I was just there, not asleep, not alive, and not dead. Just there! I knew my body was lying on my bed but my soul was on the bottom of the river bed and then I felt like I was in the corner of my room watching my half-conscious tortured soul. I cried endlessly when I was awake because I couldn't comprehend what was happening to me, and I couldn't tell anyone. I was watching myself drowning, in my dreams and in my wakened state. This went on for days.

A nurse would come to visit every day, mostly they were pleasant and chatty. They would check the drains, measure the contents then empty them. They would ask me how I was feeling, some days I tried to explain that I couldn't stop crying and that I was having weird dreams, although I never went into detail. The nurse suggested it was just my body reacting to the anaesthetic, that it could make you feel down. I said "ok" to the nurse but I knew it was more than that. They suggested it could be the medication, and changed it. It made no difference. On other days I never even tried to explain, I just let them do their job and then leave. Eight days after this all began the nurse informed me they could remove the tubes. After they had been removed I finally felt some sense of relief from the them being attached to me.

A long soak in the bath was what I needed. I had only been able to give myself some attempt at a flannel wash. Except for the night Joseph had helped me wash my hair. So I ran a bath, and slowly undressed. I stepped into the bath, the warmth of the water felt instantly soothing. I tentatively slithered into the water. It felt strange and wonderful all at the same time. I lay down and my arms and chest went beneath the water, its warmth washing over my scarred body, cleansing the iodine and dried blood away. I could feel that presence that had become familiar to me. Myself in the corner observing, I tried to ignore it and slowly lowered my head beneath the water. I lay there and something extraordinary happened. I was there on the bottom of the river bed, and I heard a familiar voice clearly say these words..."You are your own answer!! You need to write!!"

It was the same voice I had heard many times; it was the same presence I had felt in the daffodil field. As I heard it my body jerked from off the river bed and I swam, I swam with aplomb straight to the top. As I emerged from the river and my head finally came out of the water, I sprung up out of the bath water. I breathed deep filling my lungs with air. When my body dashed out the river water I felt free, free from pain, free from everything. I jumped out the bath, dried myself quickly and began to write. I stayed up late into the night writing. I wrote a book about the journey I had been on.

When I slept I dreamt of an Owl. I was standing at the end of a tree lined street, it was silent and serene. Sat perched in a hollow of an old lusciously green tree directly in front of me, was a small beautiful white Owl looking towards me. On her face were a few flecks of brown feathers, she had an adoringly mythical look about her. The Owl flew out of the tree and glided on to my shoulder. She rubbed her exceptionally soft face against mine, and I could feel it so warm and gentle. Then she whispered into my ear a similar message, in that familiar voice... 'You own your answer'.

The next morning when I lay in my bed not quite awake, although awake enough to feel. I felt all the heaviness I carried in my heart from my entire life-long journey was gone, I had left them on the bottom of the river bed. Everything, from my parents, to Jack and anything in-between! My heart didn't feel glued together like it used to, no longer mutilated by the heart breaks I had endured. It felt new and clear. All the inflictions I had been carrying around, even the ones I thought I had dealt with were gone. I felt a profound forgiveness for the human errors other people had placed on me. I understood how the ego can control you and take over you without you even knowing it. I forgave my father for all his mistakes, I now understood his mind had been controlled by his ego, my mum's mistakes too. I forgave Jack for all he had done wrong, even the pain he had and still was inflicting my family with. He too was controlled by his ego, he too, like so many human beings struggled to live beyond the mind. I accepted that our love had been pure and true once. Once it had been a love forged on our energy vibrating at the same frequency. Something untainted, along our own unique experiences our energy began to vibrate at a different frequency and then that love became convoluted. I now accepted that Jack was on his own unique path and I am on mine. I cannot walk in his shoes and understand his choices, just like no one can walk in mine. In that moment I said a final goodbye to the man I had once loved and the pain I had once felt. I had been carrying pain around that I had unnecessarily endured, I had only been hurting myself living with this remnant pain from the past. If someone hurts you, in that moment you are hurt. Carrying it around only hurts you again, and only you, not the person who caused you pain. More importantly I forgave myself for any of the egotistical decisions I had made in my past. When I had let my ego rule my being, for my own human error caused by my lack of understanding my own mind, and for not believing in myself before.

I am a part of the environment I live, and have lived. I was born into a world that some people cannot understand, but this had been my life. It was not something I chose; it was not something I consciously decided was the life I had wanted to live. It just was what it was. For better or worse I was a part of it, in as much as another life was not an option. That is until this experience showed me that I did have a choice. The decisions I had made before in my life had been infiltrated by others, but no longer. Now I am liberated from my past. Free to be me!

I felt reborn.

As my eyes flickered to open I experienced something amazing, I felt - and I felt it! The beginning of existence. That atomic explosion that produced the beginnings of the universe. It was like an eruption within me that I felt rather than I viewed. Suddenly my mind was awash with an array of knowledge, some of it things I had never contemplated before, information brimming over. It was like a dam had erupted in my mind, and its contents rushed rapidly out. I jolted upright as my being began to try and process what was happening. Over the next few days my mind was full of information swirling and swirling around, I never even imagined my mind could possibly hold so much knowledge before but it all felt so natural. I viewed the physics of the universe in a way I had never even thought about. I felt I understood that speed of light moves relative only to the person who is within the individual moment. Example; a man can struggle to find hours in the day for the many things he has to do; he works from home on his computer. The time flies past him so fast he wishes for more hours. A lady who lives right next door to him, in the same time frame, sits all day as the time drags from one minute to the next. Then there is the space, space in between two worlds, her space and his. Space and time are interlinked into one, space-time. Things that happen at the same time for one person could happen at a different time for another. I got the $E=Mc^2$, energy equals mass speed of light. Your core energy places images into your mind's eye, and then the reflection from the speed of light brings you the reality you see around you. Without that speed of light reflection, and the images your energy places in your mind there would be nothing. Nothingness! A void! I understood that without 'nothing', there cannot be 'something'. Without 'something', there cannot be 'nothing'. Experience of live is a gift, from 'ourselves' to 'ourselves', and that ourselves is 'our' 'selves'. We are all one life, connected and born from one source. Energy! The Creator! We stand as individual parts of the 'whole' to experience the 'whole', because if you are God, you cannot experience God unless you stand apart from it. To know what you are not, in order to know what you are. Einstein's mind interested me immensely, granted I have always had a fondness for intelligent men, but I liked his theory on other matters too. Like his belief on religion, a cosmic religion. His view that scientific elements of the universe could not have come about without feeling, that feeling was needed to bear fruitfulness. As in the big bang couldn't have happened without some element of feeling/emotion from something...god. That God did not punish and reward people, that people punish and reward themselves.

I had some understanding of quantum entanglement. A developmental process that occurs as particles interact with different particles and mix together, then separate, forming new ones. The very essence of evolution. I understood how gases merge and form to make planets and stars. The moon began to amaze me, her perfect alignment and its satellite powers on earth. The more I discovered about her the more important she became to me. I had never really thought about the moon in this way before, I had only ever admired her. The moon controls the waters of the earth, the ebb and flow of all waters. Up to sixty percent of humans are made up of water. The moon orbits in the same time frequency as women's menstrual cycle. It must have an effect on us if more than half of our body mass is water, it must have an effect on us women if it orbits at a time frequency that is the same as our cycle. It's amazingly accurate positioning in space, if it was closer the tides would be too high and earth would become flooded. If it was further away it would become too dry, and earth could not sustain life. Its entire infrastructure convincing me that it's perfect positioning is concrete evidence God does exist.

I saw religion for what it was, and I'm not talking about God because as far as I could see religion is far removed from what God gifted us with. Religion is the word of others. An ideology formed by men to control the mass population, used to instil a belief system of control and punishment. Religion proclaims to be the righteous path to the kingdom of heaven. When from what I could see now, was far from righteous. The words of the sacred have been rewritten to suit, yet beyond the attached infiltrated manipulations of others is a core message. Whatever belief system you follow the core message is the same; love and unity. Jesus, Buddha, Mohammed, Krishna, they are one and the same message. Every other story added on to their legend over time may be myths; but the core message is concurrent, "Love!" the most powerful, sacred emotion we are gifted with. That concurrent message isn't punish and reward, it's 'love'. Yourself, your neighbour, the planet, everything.

If you cannot believe you have been deceived through religion take a look at a relatively new religion, Scientology. Millions of people are followers, millions. In this day and age people are willing to sign up to a religion that believes you sign your soul over to it for a billion years, I don't know if that's an American billion or a British one, either way it's a hefty amount of years to sign up for. This religion was made up by a man who wrote science-fiction novels. Millions of people follow this religion, believing in the word of someone else. Where exactly L Ron Hubbard gained this information, or how the rules of this religion were concocted I'm sure only their leaders know. This though has no real difference to how other religions are projected. You do as your leaders say, you behave as you should. You live an existence based on your next life, eternal salvation. You shouldn't be true to yourself, only to religion. Your existence is about your next move, not about now. You can never know the extent of what leaders know unless you work to become one. Follow!! Follow!! Follow!! All religion seems to be is political.

Ask yourself; is it possible that modern Christianity was constructed by elitists who took fragments from old religions, fragments they merged as part of a Machiavellian master plan of formulating a systematic organisation to control? If you know the answer is yes, then everything you may have been made to believe is true isn't! *The most useful piece of learning is to unlearn what is untrue!!*

That's not a scary concept, it's a liberating one. If God wanted control of us, then we would not have been gifted with a mind of our own. Spirituality is non-political. Faith in something is your choice. Stipulation in what you have faith in is not.

"*God handed down the truth, the Devil said let's organise it* "".

Each individual has the right to free choice, and the right to carve out their own path.

'The lips of the righteous teach many, but fools die for want of wisdom. The rich man's wealth is in the City, the righteous' wealth is in his Holy place. Destruction of the poor is in their poverty; destruction of soul is in vanity...' (18) **Bob Marley**

The righteous' wealth *is* in their Holy place. Yes, it is! The rich man's wealth *is* in the city! Elitist leaders destroy us with poverty whilst they live in opulence, they control what we live. And vanity *is* destroying our souls. As I look around at what society has become, or in reality, just an extreme version of what it has always been. It's harsh! The violence on our streets, the murders and massacres that governments, terrorists and young blood thirsty brainwashed children bring. The depraved world of child abuse that has been so rife and deceptively hidden in the world of entertainment or any other position of power and the cover-ups that have gone along with these. All the cover-ups society will never know about. Cover ups like this that no one talks about; in 1999 a civil court unanimously found US local, federal and state government had conspired with members of the Mafia to assassinate Martin Luther King Jnr. The government was found guilty of the assassination of Martin Luther King Jnr over fifteen years ago and main stream media did not cover this atrocity. And by the way they also found James Earl Ray was set up. But who cares? No one it appears! All that we do know about is a minute percent of the true extent of corruption within those in positions of power. Positions in society, a society they are meant to protect.

Then you have the corruptive world of marketing and advertising, a world that is manipulating the minds of individuals with false proclamations, whilst pharmaceutical conglomerates rake in from this deception. Moulding us all into robots! We have the insatiably hungry destructive world of banking and finance, where bankers gamble our money on a whim, lose it to no consequence other than their extortionate bonuses. Then there's the media who play a vital role in feeding people with propaganda omitting the truth about what is happening in the world. In the US six corporations control 90% of the media; six corporations have control over thousands of publications that are sold to millions of ordinary people, daily. These nefarious corporations feed people information they want you to hear about, they leave the truth to come out years down the line when no one appears to care. Politicians are puppets controlled by these corporations, there to start wars just to gain control of oil fields, having you believe the war is necessary because the other country is about to obliterate us with nuclear bombs. Oh sorry they got it wrong, let's all forget about that and let's all let it happen again, what's the harm...innocent people die or suffer, the government has no issue with that.

As tiresome as it can be to truly see what is happening in our world, if we don't change things there will be no world left to tire of. Each person can do something to change this, become aware. Share your awareness, remain calm and peaceful so that together our world can find an answer to the destructive path that lays ahead if this world continues as it is.

For far too long the world has put more obstacles in the way of women than it has for men. Women were once revered, she was a life giver and childbirth was a mystery and we were worshipped because of this, until we gradually lost our freedom and became subordinate and inferior to men. Women all across the world feel undervalued; marginalised, sexualised and unheard. Women in general do not see the power we hold as a collective. Women should collect in their chosen professions and begin their own thing. Political party - it is not impossible to begin a new political party. Imagine the instant following you could gain, if approached in a truly feminist way, with true equality, judging someone on merit not gender. The music and film industry – all the strong women you see amongst them, those who aren't afraid to be who they are, if they stood together and built something that gives other women a fair chance, a chance to achieve all that they know they can. Business in all forms could begin again. Let's face it the world's fucked under the control of men, who still carry around 'cock-envy' the underpinning of their current dilemma. Women should give it a go. Collect, thrash out all those ideas, compromise where necessary so that you can work in harmony with each other to achieve what all those men who know; that if women realise the power we have if we stand together as an entire collective, then men would truly have the rug pulled from under them. Perhaps then men could see if we all work together, equally benefiting each other's strengths, then a change would come. Right now men rule with control and power, and it's not getting us anywhere good. You would only believe that equality truly exists if you are male, because all women feel it, know it does not. We have to fight for our rights. We have to become someone else to prove we can do what men can do. We forget we are not men, and that we don't really need to try and be them. The point of Yin and Yang is that there are two opposites that work in harmony. It is not the historic transgression of Yang being superior to Yin as it is foretold in Confucianism. This is a misconception. To work in harmony, you need an acceptance of difference and a quantified equality of those differences. In 'The I Ching' it states; *when society observes their proper rights and place the cosmos remained stable. But if the rights and roles are transgressed then heaven would wreak havoc in the form of famine, plague and political collapse.* Well look around, it's happening. In my interpretation of those words it's not about being subordinate to anyone, and staying in your place. It's about being true to who you are and not verging away from that. For then there is harmony within. *As within, so without*! Acceptance of what one can do and what one cannot do is how we can work in harmony with our opposites.

Men have ruled and they have directed our path for too long. From the beginning of what is historically recorded, and I say historically recorded because when a woman has made a powerful difference she has been vilified or eradicated from our history books. It's up to the women of the world to stand up for their rights and find inspiration in the many, many historic women who have shined a light on the path to true equality. Men have been the leading force behind all exterior choices put on society. They may not have inflicted your being internally, but if men have never inflicted, in any form, the direction of your journey so far, then you are either very young or you live alone on a deserted island. Male leaders, male bosses, male religious leaders, male hero's, male's singing *"It's a man's world"*. Does anyone ever mention it was a woman who wrote the first novel, or first designed the computer, or touch-tone telephones, 'frequency hopping' - the foundations of Wi-Fi, even beer. No because no one cares, men made the electric light to take us out of the dark, that's all that matters. No one ever sings about the true inflictions women have had placed upon them, how to get anywhere in life you need to get through a barrage of men. In whatever form that be found in. Personally! Professionally! Emotionally! Physically! Thousands of years ago in Vietnam two sisters' regained power they had felt was taken from women by men. Vietnam was a place that once held true to the equality of female and male, until men eradicated this. The Trung Sisters gave them a run for their money, sadly it wasn't to last. Chinese Emperors invaded taking power once again, killing everyone in their way. I am not negative towards men; how can I be I have three beautiful sons. I'm just viewing the truth as a woman and you guys have stood in our way for far too long. If we are rich or poor! Beautiful or societies version of 'ugly'! Fat or thin! If we are clever and driven, we are mocked as hard bitches. If we are vulnerable, we are taken advantage of. If we have an amazing body and pretty face we are exploited. If we can sing, we are sold down the river to a music industry that sexualises all young talented women. If we can act - the equally 'man-made' industry undervalues our talents next to our male counterpart. Whatever your life, whatever path you take, men always stand judging you as a woman. Not as an individual. Not as an equal.

Women most certainly are not alone in their endurance of oppression. Homosexual people, black people, poor people, witches, anything that does not fit into the elitist perception of being superior. Africans were seen as the beginning of humanity, yet they too were not equal. Not in western society anyway. Long ago a new world began one where humans colonised. The trade of human slaves across the Atlantic was vast, deadly, and torturous and lasted hundreds of years. People who believed in oneness, people who shared what they had with their neighbour were herded up like cattle and removed from their native land, tortured and controlled to do whatever was asked of them. They were programmed to forget their native land, forget their native traditions and leave behind the beliefs and faiths they held dear. Native Indians where driven out, Aborigines too. Armies took control of land their Emperors' desired, through any means necessary. Homosexuals have always been oppressed, unless you were a Samurai or a Gladiator. Class difference and native origin give weight to the significance of the world you exist in. So called lower classes have long been held in an oppressive state. Witches were burnt for believing in something that went against the grain of religious beliefs; millions of women over hundreds of years were killed by the Holy Inquisition. Women were accused of witch craft for nothing more than loving animals, walking alone in the fields gathering medicinal plants. Burned at the stake for this! Millions of women, yet these were not recorded as a profound human crime. This still goes on today in some remote parts of the world, the mind boggles.

For me, as I viewed all this I knew I needed to be strong...and believe in *myself*. I cannot change the choice of anyone but myself, and I chose with an awakened mind to change myself. I am free to make my own choices. I am free! It feels good. I know what has gone on before me, what is going on around me. The only thing I have the power to do something about though is to change myself. I am hopeful my children will walk in a world where we are capable of standing together as equals, as neighbours on a very small part of the entire universe. Together as 'one'! White, black, rich, poor, gay, straight, fat, thin, without these labels. Just as who we are. To 'just be'. I am also hopeful some of these strong young intelligent women or men will be brave enough to stand up and be counted, and lead the world to a peaceful, harmonious state. One thing that is needed from women is to be capable of equality themselves, sadly society has brainwashed far too many women so much that we don't endorse other women's strengths, we berate and negate them. Women are women's worst critics, sadly. To empower another female, you have to empower yourself as a female first. Time for a change I think!

In this day and age life is filled with something always going on, never in history have we had so many devises to so called make our lives simpler, yet it's full of more frustration than ever before. Lives are full, but lives are empty. People measure time, they live for the next moment, they don't realise they aren't living anymore. They don't see the true beauty all around. They are too busy checking what everyone else is doing via social networks. A bird is free to fly! A bird is free to sing! A bird is free...so can you be! I am glad that I can now see the truth of this power crazy world we inhabit, so that I can make choices based on what I know to be true, not choices that have been indoctrinated into my mind.

On top of this knowledge, some of which I had never previously contemplated, I felt a complete oneness with the universe. My soul had taken me through the most amazing experience of my life and I understood that my energy field vibrates through the universe, entwined into every other living thing. I wanted to be outdoors amongst nature, to experience the beauty all around me. The trees, I looked upon their beauty at the different shades of bark and the knots and twists that feed into the earth surrounding the trees. The entire infrastructure of a tree amazed me, how a small seed contained all the knowledge it needs to grow into a magnificent long-lasting, deep rooted presence. The birds, the plants, and the grass that was greener than I had ever seen it. Everything took on a vibrant glow. The colours, the shape and the smell of the flowers entranced me. The sky in the day and at night, the vast space out there, the twinkling stars, some of whom died a long time ago and the endless planets we cannot even see. The beauty that shone from people astounded me. My new awakened view on the world was electrifying. I wanted, and did, walk bare foot on the grass, a need to feel the soles of my feet on the earth below. I was completely euphoric. Elation beyond imagination encompassed my soul. I would say I couldn't believe how happy I was but that would be untrue...it felt like home! This was the ultimate soulful experience of my entire journey. I began to see the possibilities the universe had to offer me, instead of the impossibilities the world had so far put in front in my way.

'I want to write the unrightable wrong...for I dare to dream the impossible dream' ((19))

I became aware of my own mortality, and I knew I didn't want to leave this existence without every trying. I didn't want to just survive I wanted to live. On my own terms, in a manner I deemed good enough. My journey through life nearly destroyed me, I had come to a point of no return...or so I had thought. I was floored and my soul left me...so that I could find me. Then I was reborn. Now I am brave enough to dream. Dream of achieving something I know is within me.

As a child I had dreamt of a better life. Once I had thought Jack was my better life, I was wrong, yet I was right. He gave me the three greatest gifts anyone could every give me. He also gave me enough pain to push me into the light. My dream of a better life meant I had to go through all I had been through to get to the other side. I had to endure those dramas so I could take myself to an all-encompassing me, the best version of all I could be. This was what I had felt in the daffodil field, this is why I had taken every turn I had.

So my journey became a different one, it became a journey of spirituality, a journey of self-belief and faith. I was going to follow my heart, and listen to the voice that had been guiding me all along, even at times when I wasn't listening, it was there. Now that voice was something I would listen to, always! I believed in the dream I had of succeeding to become a published writer, and I was willing to carry on working towards that dream until I succeeded. I was completely in tune to all inspiration, I was aware of every little thing that was presenting itself to me. The ideas for stories just kept coming and I began writing them. I had no fear of ridicule, or rejection, or failure because the ability to 'try', for the first time in my life, removed any emotion attached to ridicule, rejection, or failure. I had finally discovered what was in my heart and I was now willing to act upon it. Life would never be the same again.

Chapter Twelve

A new day dawned, a bright new day. I rose from my bed with the energy of life emanating from within me. I now had a deep sense of peaceful joy, one that before this experience I had never felt in my life before. Except I believe a brief glimpse of what was to come when I was a child sitting in the Daffodil field. I pulled on my dressing gown and slid my feet into my slippers, and then I went down the stairs into my kitchen. I filled the kettle and made myself a cup of tea. I leant my back against the work top, cup nestled into my chest and I watched the blue sky outside. The birds flying by and the white clouds passing over, my mind was fresh and clear. For the first time in my life my mind, body and soul were aligned. My entire journey through life had led me to this place I now found myself in, a soulful existence. I drank my tea and just watched, completely immersed in the 'Now'. It was a wondrous feeling.

My scars were healing nicely and soon I would return to work, right now though nothing mattered.

Then I heard footsteps coming down the stairs and my attention turned to my boys.
"Morning mummy!" said Dj as he bounced up into my arms.
"Morning beautiful" I replied.
"I'm hungry!"
"You're always hungry my boy!" I laughed.
"Come on I'll get you some cereal." I lifted him up onto the kitchen unit and got his bowl out. I looked adoringly at my sleepy little boy with his hair all over the place and the cheeky grin he always wore. It was his smile that had saved me in my darkest hour. I didn't realise it at the time, but looking back so much is clear to me. In the days before I truly stepped onto my spiritual path, the days when darkness was on the verge of taking over my being. It was his wonderfully beautiful smile that he gave to me every morning that he woke beside me. A sweet little innocent two-year-old baby, in his cosy stripy pyjamas, his blonde wispy hair flapping about on the pillow, and he would smile his beautiful smile. They will always remain the best smiles of my life, because they kept away the darkest thoughts of my mind. Thoughts that could take hold and that would come to me in the wake of every morning.
I kissed my sweet boy, and poured his cereal.

There was no magical wand waved, I didn't magically find myself in a new home, where all our problems ended. I was still in the house, and the repossession was still going ahead. I also still had to get myself back to work - the mundane practicalities ever present. What did happen was I felt peace deep inside and was ready to go down a tunnel I thought had no end, one I believed I could never get out from. Now I walked through it with true honest faith that I would find my way.

Before my operation I had begun packing all our belongings up, all that had been put on the back burner whilst I dealt with the current situation. Now it was time to fully embrace this new chapter in life. So I began the search for a new home, confident - even after some of the damp filled, filthy houses I viewed - that we would find the right home, and it would be one that was bright and clean. One that was ready to take me to the next chapter... I fully intended and was completely confident that I would become a published writer. My new start was just the next step of the journey.

The months passed by, I went back to my job, and I continued looking for a new home. I was in no rush to choose one that wasn't right for us, I still had not heard from the courts with a date, and I was aware that these things can take time. Before I knew it Christmas was upon me, as the children and I put the decorations up in the house I had spent seventeen years in, I knew it would be the last. I knew that the new start I needed was just around the corner. A week before Christmas I got news about a home we had viewed, a bright, clean home. It would be available in the New Year. How apt I thought, New Year, new start and all that. Early January had always been a starting or an ending point for things with me, this was both.

The boys and I enjoyed our Christmas, it felt like things had finally taken a turn towards that new chapter I desperately wanted to take us all to. I wanted to one day buy a home with enough space for all of our needs. I needed to feel financially secure. I never wanted to feel that stress I had felt again. I no longer wanted to stress about finding money for the mundane things I had been struggling to afford; bus fare, food, heating. General things had become something I struggled for, daily, and it had become very difficult to accept. When my growing boys needed clothes or something else I considered going back to my days as a thief, but that moment passed as quickly as it came. My friends knew how much I was struggling, they could tell. They would offer to help, and I accepted where I could. They didn't bare any responsibility to my family though and there was only so much they could give. I accepted that this was where I was meant to be and had faith that I could succeed on my own. I wanted my own home. In my name that no one could ever take away from us. I would get there of that I was confident. I was too hungry to fail.

I had written a children's story about two young boys - inspiration I got from my little boy and his cousin. It was about two little Superhero's and the journey they went on. Along the way they learnt many things, and grew confident in their own abilities. It was a fun, adventurous tale. A friend of mine, Richy (JP's Dad) drew some illustrations. Another friend, Sarah (JP's sister) bound it into a book for me. That family have been a blessing to my life, and I will be forever grateful. I gave it to lots of different people to read, the feedback was so positive it gave weight to my own confidence in it. Then I started sending it out to publishing companies, which I learnt is a long path of patience.

So in the New Year our family closed the door on the cloud that had been hanging over us, the devastation Jack had caused our lives was for me removed. For my children it was partially removed, he is their father and it is something they may always have issues around. They will possibly always look upon other fathers who they see with their own son's with a heavy heart. Until they alleviate that pain with having their own children, like I did. I am hopeful that the work I had always put into their upbringing and the work I would infinitely apply to them, that their pain would never be more than it had to be. Or rather it could be addressed and accepted, without them allowing it to infiltrate who they are. From suffering you can learn, I know this will make them amazing father's themselves one day, father's that treasure their own children.

The mortgage company sent a lock-smith to the house and as I handed him the keys I felt relief. The weight had been lifted off my shoulders and I could begin my life anew. I felt no sadness as I left, even though it had been all my children's first home, and the happy memories that had occurred there, because the times in my life were I had suffered most had been there. It had caused me so much pain in the last few years, the weight of it hanging around me had felt like a noose around my neck, and now it was gone. In the last few months before I left everything had started to break, the taps, my bed had been destroyed by endless wrestling - unfortunately not from me, but my three sons - the door handles on nearly every door had come off, the shower...it was as if the house was telling me to go.

I unpacked my things in my new home and a deep sense of peace was present within me. I knew this was the right move for my family. With it I wanted to leave behind anything negative that had attached itself to me, it was for my own well-being. Over the years it has been since Jack turned his back on my family I had heard things about him, been drawn into conversations around him. Always negative. Now I couldn't ever hear any more about what his choices were. I had forgiven his human errors, but I could no longer be any part of such negativity. So I turned a new corner, a bright positive corner. In my new bedroom I painted the walls, put my new bed together. My belongings fitted in perfectly, my new bedroom was full of positive energy and I loved it.

As for my books, I discovered that to succeed you must laboriously strife through all that stands in your way. It is not an easy journey; it requires serious amounts of self-belief, and endless amounts of time on the chosen project. My books were rejected by every publishing company I sent them to. I had positive feedback, but still it was a no. Every time I would get back to it and send it to other publishers. After a while it began to get to me. A low point would come over me and I would wonder what I was doing wrong, I had been pro-active, positive, and confident. What? Just as this low point would come over me another inspiration would come, a new idea, a new story. Every time I would realise that if I had succeeded in one thing, this next inspiration may not have come. So for a few years this is what happened, rejected by publishers, a low point, and a new inspiration. Then back at it, back trying. I never felt low for too long, and my suffering was never again with the extremity it had been on the many occasions of sadness I had felt before I had that beautiful experience. Day to day life had taken away the intensity, but it was still there. My heart was still fresh, past inflictions had been removed forever.

After another venture I had tried still did not bring fruition I was inspired to try something else. This inspiration came when I had a problem in work that brought a chance for me I didn't see coming. Without innate details I witnessed some negligence that when reported was brushed under the carpet by managers who should have had more integrity. My morals wouldn't allow me to stay with them, and my Liverpool ethic of nongrassing left me with no choice but to hand my notice in without reporting them further up the chain. I was fed up with the bureaucratic nonsense that these organisations have; they preach respect and honesty...so called charities, but only when it serves them. An average life wasn't what I wanted anyway; half descent job, meet a half descent guy, live a half descent life. I wanted something different, something that surpassed mediocrity. All that I had been working for is to succeed, to a place of financial security, for my children's enjoyment and my peace of mind. I worked on my books, tried new ideas believing that each one was my ticket out of the life I was living. Financially I was in the worst position I had ever been in, poverty of the purse is nothing next to poverty of the heart and I had learnt that lesson, so moments of despair passed by. Things didn't come to me like I thought they would but I knew in my heart that did not mean I should give up. The realisation I had; was that I couldn't take the huge leap I had wanted to take to achieve my dream. I had it in my head that if I done one thing amazing it would fix our financial issues, and end my dilemma. A kind soul called Andrea helped me see this; I had to take small steps. Over the last few years I had been trying to find more time to write, thinking that I could fix everything in one big leap. Even though my enlightenment is embedded within - for once it is felt it is felt - the intensity is sometimes blighted by my everyday existence, bills and money worries. Life is not just a pretty picture; it is daunting and draining sometimes. When I don't pay attention and allow the outside world to invade my being I become disconnected from the happiness I carry within, and my world feels cold. The everyday struggles I had of finding money for the things my family needed, the constant struggle to survive and the rejection from publishers was hard to bare at times, especially as I was so certain I would succeed. Yet the more I allowed that feeling to wash over me the more troubled I became. Each time I would get that feeling a clear sign would find me and make me learn from what I was feeling, bringing me back to understanding the way of the universe, guiding me back to my true happiness, and my peaceful state would step back in to greet me again.

One of those signs was that as I wasn't working...I had more time to write, time I had been looking for. So I worked on finishing some children's books I had started and finished an adult's book I had been working on. Another sign was when I got to spent a beautiful day in the park with the other lone dog walkers, and watched an eclipse. The moon in all her glory overshadowed the sun from our view on earth. It was magical. Something

I would have missed had I been working. So the inspiration I had was; small steps. As the saying goes - *Life isn't the destination, it's the journey.*

In between my writing I also enrolled onto a course gaining a diploma that qualifying me as a Life Coach. Whilst I was going through this course, and through my reading I gained something powerful. I realised why my writing had not exactly been a success up until now. I had attached too much energy towards the outcome. I had needed it to work. My entire focus had been on the future, the past I had alleviated, but I had replaced this with the future. I recognised that I had never been a forward thinker. Never had I looked too far into the future, maybe if I had I would have seen the obvious things going on in my life, but I hadn't. Some people in life are chess players, planning their moves ten steps ahead. I'm not one of them, and I can't be what I am not. I am an observer, not a planner. When I had tried to look to the future it hadn't happened, because that's not part of my unique experience. Everyone is different, some people need to manoeuver their way through. I finally understood I wasn't one of them. Now I get it, the penny dropped. The only real thing...IS NOW! This present moment! Live it, breathe it, and experience its wondrous beauty for what it is. Now! My way is to just follow the path I am on, the way of the universe. Everyone's way is unique to who they are and what they are here to experience. So mine is not the manifestational way of living, it's to follow the signs on the path I have chosen way, and just roll with it.

So I detached myself from the outcome, I didn't *need* it. I didn't give up on my dreams I merely readjusted my thought process. I still desired it, I still worked towards it. I just worked towards it in the *now.* I still believed in my dreams, but I discovered the joy of all the moments that occur along the way, learning from the experience it was giving me. I consciously let go of what the end result would be.

And then it all just came...

Last chapter

The dense heat catches my breath as I step out of the plane and onto the metal staircase, my eyes slowly take in the new country I have never before had the pleasure of visiting. The sun is setting on the scene before me that brings those beautiful orange and red hues to the sky. It casts a mellow vibration that waves past me and through me. I breathe a deep happy sigh and smile, Francis and Joseph are in front of me and Dj is holding my hand. My mum and Anthony follow.

It never really hit me until we walked around the corner of an average European street, all quaint cafes and expensive little boutiques. Straight into the Pantheon, it came right out of nowhere. The grey, dark, round building looms monstrously in the middle of the small streets that surround it, yet it's there and it's been there long before the streets. The entrance is as enormous as you can imagine. Huge columns that stand before the mammoth wooden doors, I walked in and observed the round building, the decor gold and brown marble. There are statues and paintings of people I have never heard of, there's this alter relating to such-and-such and a shrine for someone else. I start to look around for some Masonic symbols, thinking I can find the things I read about in a book once. I'm looking at crosses and small symbols pondering about 'it must be something'. Then I get a grip of myself and remember I have no fucking clue what a Masonic symbol looks like. So I move on to look at a huge painting of some priest whom I suspect would have known about the Masonic symbolism that abounds the entire city. The next corner brings mountainous columns and enormous white sleek roman buildings. My mum had brought us all to Rome, her treat and some unsaid way of saying sorry I guess. My mum has turned a massive corner in her life. She had an epiphany or a nightmare or something and it altered her perception on her life. But that's her story, and her part in my story has been whatever it has been. Within that year, the worst financially I ever had my mum helped me, helped my family get through. She is in a much happier place and I love seeing her glow. She no longer looks beaten when I look in her eyes, she has something shining in there and it's a wonderful thing to see. No matter what our relationship has been in the past, it looks positive from here on in. She is my mum and she has had her own share of lessons to learn. I'm proud she turned that corner. And I love her, I always have and I always will.

The enormity of the relics that stand before your eyes in Rome immediately drag your mind to a place that existed a long, long, time ago; the men in the finest red velvet toga's and gold leaf wreath resting on their heads, whilst being carried around on their opulent thrones by slaves, the Praetorian Guards gallantly protecting their Emperor. Rome is full of history more than any other place I have been before, and the history in the big scheme of things wasn't that long ago. History of how creating a belief in something can cause catastrophic events still felt today. Mum took us to the Vatican; somewhere she has always wanted to go, where the vast, seriously unchristian opulence and the awe inspiring craftsmanship blew me away equally. It's so big, so clean and shiny. Marble, everything looks marble. There is vast art work of paintings that will have been done by the hand of some creative genius hundreds of years ago. Statues and shrines of saintly people, some of whom I have heard of. In the midst of it all is a gold and black raised throne, that is so big and opulent it's monstrous to look at. How can the world contain so much poverty, yet the church of Christianity has so much wealth? Joseph starts telling me about the story of Jesus, and how he rejected wealth. He understands the contrast of what we are looking at and what is portrayed as Christian. From the words of 'John the Baptist': *"Whoever has two coats must share with someone who has none, and the same with food."* I think the Vatican forgot about the teachers they proclaim to follow.
There is an embalmed Pope laying in a glass coffin which I have to explain to Dj that it's just pretend, whilst his brothers laugh at my words. Dj decides to fart mid conversation for all to hear, his brothers laugh a little louder. Well if God lived in a house like this, he's just let the crazy crew enter through his doors. We visited the Sistine Chapel, and viewed the story of Moses and the story of Christ painted along the walls of this historic Chapel. Then you look up and see the amazing work of Michelangelo's. The hand of God reaches out from the cloudy perch his body rests upon whilst entangled in the midst of Angels, towards the hand of Adam, Michelangelo's interpretation of the moment of God's creation of the first man on earth. Definitely things to remember, if it wasn't so Christian I would have enjoyed it more. I did love the out buildings that surround the Vatican, inside Vatican City. Little chapels and houses sat in the middle of such landscaped perfection.
We ate amazing food the entire holiday, in the Plaza Navona we all sat looking over at the spectacular fountain, it's called Fontana dei Quattro Fiumi - the Fountain of the Four Rivers. It is a large beautiful fountain that is encircled with four white stone carved godly looking men sitting naked

in a confident pose upon the huge rocks that elevate them to give the appearance of supreme beings; one knee up, one leg further out, arm resting on the bent knee, very masculine, very Roman. It was a wonderful place to stop and eat, the water from the fountains glistened in the sun. It was so hot it did look inviting but when Dj wanted to get naked and jump in we only just managed to stop him, just. The food was fit of a King; Francis ate everything he could. He is now addicted to a Cannoli's. Mamma-mia!! We all loved the Coliseum; you can hear the roar from the mass of people that would have sat in the seats surrounding the arena, and the men that would have come through the large gates to bravely face their death. The mind conjures up images of Gladiators having to fight each other or wild beasts, just to entertain. The history of the place has me thinking the world has been fucked up for too long. Men kill men for political reasons, cultural, religious, survival, power, respect...for fun. All battles born in the ego, all! Does anyone really have the justification to take another person's life? I think not, not for war, not for justice, not for any reason. One killing doesn't justify another. Hopefully the world we live in will one day seek a life of peace and togetherness, hopefully...one day. For now, in this moment, our holiday was amazing. Full of fun and togetherness, oh and lots of food. It was a much deserved time for this family of mine. The nicest day we had was spent looking for the Spanish Steps, Anthony who always had a habit of taking us on missions of discovery through many muddy fields, translated - he always got us lost. In-fact I think it's in the blood, whenever we go for a walk up hills and mountains Francis has a habit of taking us off the beaten track into a muddy world that brings great views one would not discover on the beaten track. So we stumbled into a park, an Italian park on a Sunday in the centre of Rome. Where families spent quality time together playing; they sped past on Segway's, they rode bikes around the park together, they played football, flew kites and they ate. Lots of eating! We joined in, what a world away from where my family are from. We sat on benches eating sandwiches bought from a van, that where better than most sandwiches I had ever tasted. The part of the park we had chosen to stop at was raised, so our view was the roof tops of Rome. All manner of topping, the orange red of terracotta, the browns and the greys of the different roofs, stacked up in different heights and angles, old mixed in with new. Lots of domes scattered about. It was a perfect day. European's have such a beautiful outlook on family life. I love it.

After we returned I came up with a new plan, I had been writing stories, trying to get them published for many years. The new book I had been working on was a different story. It was my own. It was important to me. I had a 'fuck it' moment. Going through publishers was laborious, and because of the vast number of submissions made to publishing companies, it was extremely hard to break through. So I figured I might as well try and self-publish it. Why not I asked myself, what have I got to lose? I had nothing to lose. So I grafted day after day, writing it, fixing it, rewriting it, re-fixing it. It was cathartic to get it all down on paper. To release it. Then I came to the end. So the next step on my journey is to put it out there. So I did. I had qualified as a life coach, and was earning enough money to live not just survive. Then I sat back and took it all in.

A few months later I was sat on a train to London. A publisher had discovered my book. When the next point came…the point of sitting in that office waiting I felt serenity breath in and out of every pore on my body. Everything's going to alright! Everything is alright! My faith just rewarded me, big time! My search to attain a better future for my family was found. After all my hard work, not just writing my books and sending them off, but the long process that is part of achieving ones dream. The self-belief needed to never give up, and the fortitude to try something different. It takes determination to achieve a dream, the dream you know you must attain, for it is in your soul. Now it has arrived! Step by step I got to where I wanted to go.

So when I finally secured that lucrative book deal, everything I had faith in was rewarded. My dreams came true when I walked into the book store and my books sat on their shelves.

I knew how much I had learnt from all the experiences of my journey, and I knew I wouldn't be who I am without them. I learnt to let go, I learnt I had once lived a life based on pain caused in my past. Forgiveness came to bless me, and with it came acceptance, of all that had been and all that would come. I learnt acceptance of life, the everyday moments, moments that are sad, happy, annoyed, loving, whatever they are I accept them. I discovered that the seeker I had once been, the person seeking spiritual enlightenment already had all the answers within, nothing was gained externally. I learnt love and unity and to live in the 'Now'. I learnt to trust in my own word and follow the ways of the universe. I found happiness and peace, to carry me along the rest of my journey; to continue growing and learning from the experience's life shows me, and to share my knowledge with my children, the ones that choice to walk beside me. The ones that gave me strength in every moment.

My beautiful children have grown so much. Francis is eighteen. He has an apprenticeship and is doing his own thing in life, girls, drinking, and his friends. All the things an eighteen-year-old should be doing. He has dealt with what his dad has done to him, as much as he can. He is a very good person, and I am blessed to have him. He's determined, driven, stoic and seriously stubborn. Yet soft and calm, he does things I guide him not too; like fall out with his dad's family, although he was trying to protect me and I admire him for that. That is his decision though and I am always there to stand beside him no matter what happens. *A lie really does travel faster than the truth!* The one's that believe those lies fall prey to making decisions not from true facts. Jack's family are gone from our lives, and that has been no bad thing in all honesty. Negativity is not something I enjoy around us. The two younger ones still see them occasionally they enjoy their company but often return with a heavy heart. Jack's family or anyone else for that matter can never understand the pain my children feel. If a father walks out on his family and basically goes missing there is a torturous enduring pain that they carry around. He isn't dead, that would have been easier to bare. He is out there somewhere and he does not contact them, he does not show any signs of being their father. So when they watch other father's kiss their son's goodnight, or playing with their son's it hurts them, or when other little children make fun of them for not knowing where their daddy is it crushes them. When they are among Jack's family and they talk about Jack it is in a negative manner, this hurts them too. They return home full of emotion until it releases out in floods of tears. They cry for their dad. I hold them and we talk about it, then we move forward. Jack's sister and her husband try to understand. There is no text book on the right way to do things, but at least they try, and I know they love them. Francis is at a point in his life where he wants to know everything about the world, and this has me singing the same song from when I was eighteen...just a different lyric.

'...relax, take it easy! You're still young that's your fault, there's so much you have to go through...' [20] **Cat Stevens**

My beautiful Joseph with those gorgeous green eyes is a strapping thirteen-year-old young man now. He is turning into an amazing young man, like I always knew he would. He's sensitive, intelligent, and calm in nature, a deep thinker of many thoughts. He lives in a city obsessed with money and he suffered for too long, wanting what we could not afford, five hundred pound coats and goodness knows what else. Next to other thirteen-year-olds he understood his mum was trying and that I gave him all I had. Now we can afford them he doesn't get why I wouldn't spend ridiculous amounts of money on clothes, but he will one day. He still and always will love me and test me in equal quantities. He understands things way beyond his age. He is also the most audacious child on earth, corrects me when I am wrong. Even if I'm in the midst of screaming at him for whatever has gone on, he still tries to correct me. Again I am truly blessed to have him, he challenges me endlessly. He makes me laugh like no other too.

My Dj is seven-years-old and is still the craziest cat ever. He pulls funny faces, makes strange noises constantly. He farts like no other and he's the worst loser ever. He's also the cutest, cuddliest, cheekiest little monkey that blesses me every day. His suffering from his dad is now apparent when he asks me; "Do I know him? Does he know me? When did I meet him? Will he come home to me? Can you get me his number so I can call him?" How sad, a little boy of seven feels these things, but we cope. We get by. I try to be honest as I can to help him. He has yet to grasp the enormity of our situation, and when he does I will help and support him. I will ask him if he would like to learn to meditate, see if that assists him too. For in the words of Buddha when someone asked him what meditation gave him, he replied; *"Nothing, but I can tell you what it took away...anger, anxiety, depression and insecurity!"*

I look at their faces as I watch them grow, and I see the fun we have had all along the way. We have all had so much to accept on our journey, but we have always had fun too. I always felt that the happiest times we had where those spent within a complete family unit. Looking back, I was wrong, those moments in time when we were together, sharing happiness, were beautiful and joyous, but they were moments, blimps in time. It was all those times in between, those birthdays, Christmas', climbing mountains, camping in fields, lost journeys... and laughter. The many shared events – scored goals, accidents and incidents (an apple stuck in an ear, you don't want to know!) Those are what has been our life, our happy family life. Like when I convinced Francis to buy two bags of concrete at the top of the road and carry them home. We bought them, and the guy in the shop put them on Francis' shoulder. We walked out, crossed the road and Francis looked at me with urgency "Grab one..." "What?" I said. Through his gritted teeth "...grab it" and he just let it go straight through my hands splitting on the floor. He just walked off and left me, I couldn't stop laughing. I couldn't even pick it up at all. He never saw the humour till later on when his shoulder had recovered. The funniness for me was in the shop he hadn't flinched, all manly like. I thought he was alright. Once out the shop his manliness went by the wayside.

Almost daily, we sit around our table laughing. Joseph's like the jester among us. He also fills us all with knowledge about things we hadn't even considered, like the goings on of WW1, or why hippo's roam Columbia, or who exactly Pythagoras is. He is a vat of information, and he keeps us all on our toes. When we moved house Anthony and Francis were attempting to ram the couch through the door, Joseph got the measuring tape out saying "mathematically this is impossible!" We laugh at each other's silly quirks and combined weird sense of humour. Dj tops the rank for weirdness; he is a bag of craziness. Don't get me wrong, the noise levels in my house are highly uncalled for, one of them will be crying because the other one has hit them and the other one will be laughing, or they're wrestling...it drives me round the bend and at least once a day I want drop kick one of them, or all of them if they are all winding me up. But then I take myself in the garden for a ciggie and the world is well again.

When I think about it the boys and I have had a happier life than we would have had if Jack and his ego driven drama had stayed around. Over the years my little boys have had to live with me through all this, the good, the bad and the ugly. They've lived a world away from the one I envisaged for them, I've been a different parent than the one I thought I would be. I messed up sometimes, and I made wrong decisions and took a path I should have removed myself from as soon as it began. My stress over the many years of the journey to self-awareness has brought the best and worst out of me. I was unapproachably alone in my heart through some of this and that came out in negative qualities. I could be sullen and bad tempered. Or insanely stressed, methodically cleaning our home. Or I had to be overly stern thinking that was how to rear three boys

to respect me. I've punished and walked away when all I wanted to do was hug them. I've shouted when I've sometimes wanted to laugh. Believing I was doing the right thing. Those three beautiful souls have lived so much for their young age, but I understand now...that that's what makes you who you are. One lesson I teach them in words, because love, respect, honesty, togetherness come from the way our family interact with each other. I always want them to understand, they have so much to give. Everybody does. If everybody was given the chance to feel respected and loved everybody would thrive. My children will always know they have more to give than just another statistic. They can achieve whatever they are willing to work at, whatever they are willing to put their hearts into they will achieve. We're not perfect by any stretch of the imagination, they leave the toilet like a rhino's invaded sometimes. None of them know where the fucking washing basket has lived for years, or for that matter what a bin is, the washing machine, the sink. I could go on but I'll safe that for them, because as it goes I'm also a moaner. Who wants perfection though, it's surely over-rated to have a perfect world. Yet in all my worlds imperfections, all my children's imperfections and all my own imperfections I'm blessed and happy to live in my crazy world. I love every minute my Son's!
Equanimity rests within and I am free to be me. The best lesson I can ever show them. The joy of being free!

So I come to the end of my story, as I write this final chapter I have to pay homage to the experience I never would have believed I could have had; the experience that changed me. The experience that gave me answers, and gave me belief. The experience that took away the pains I had carried through my life. The experience that freed me. Words will never do justice to that experience, an experience that goes beyond reality. It turned my life around. Now I know, that the very beginning energy that omitted a flicker of something that began the universal chain of events; that beginning energy - God, part of that energy is in every living thing. It's everywhere, it's all around. For me it's the thing I sat on the river bed for days with, God! The part of my soul that is part of that beginning energy. She showed me the way, and I say she because I am female. It is whatever you are, it can't be anything else. And I learnt to listen to my own word above anyone else's, because the truth is; only 'you' truly know 'you' and only inside 'you' are the truthful answers 'you' seek.

Lots of things have assisted my journey through it all. Music has always been something that helped me, back in the day of Mel and Kim teaching me '*Respectable*' (21), to my journey with Bob about '*Turning my lights down low*' (22). *To raindrops keep falling on my head* (23)... because those blues they sent to beat me, didn't defeat me. My dream of *righting the unrightable wrong,* this song gave me courage. The world around me expected me to fall on my knees after all my tribulations but I refused to. In the words of my Grandfathers favourite singer – '*...I did what I had to do and saw it through without exemption...to say the things I truly feel, and not the words of one who kneels....*' (24)

My friends, the beautiful friendships I have; with Christine, who has helped me immeasurably throughout my many dramas. She has made me smile when I felt like I would never smile again. She has helped me stay sane, or sometimes, when needs must, be crazy. She has always been there for me regardless of the situations I have been in, and she has never judged me. Sandra who has been the big sister I never had, the one I trust with my children. The highest praise I could give to someone, is entrusting them with my children. She too has supported me, and hugged me when she could see life eating away at my soul. Paula, who has supported my many ventures and never questioned me, she has helped me whenever I have asked her and never, not once expected anything in return. Tracey, who has sat with cups of tea, or wine on better days, chatting about everything and nothing, easing the burden of the single-parent life we both live, and Stan who helped me to have faith in human's kindness. My lifelong companion, my brother Anthony, the one who has shared every moment, good and bad with me from the beginning of my time. Over the many years we have hated each other and loved each other like true siblings. We have laughed, cried, hurt each other, supported each other and are there for each other. The biggest and best thing about my brother, the thing that I will never be capable of repaying, is that he has been the constant male figure in my children's lives. The friendship he shares with them is testament to that, and the love that I have for him is forged on a lifelong bond. I don't know how I got stuck with him, he's a rolling in shit dandelion kind of guy, he knows intelligent stuff but just likes to float on by. He's a good stick at heart though. As my boy's age I'm wary of his influence; women, gambling and football. Men eh! The boys love it. The most incredible thing in my life has been my children.
My three best friends, without them I would be nothing. Only to them am I something. Without them there would have been nothing in my life

worth fighting for. They have given me strength and meaning, and love. They make me proud, make me laugh, make my heart swell, they make me the person I am. The four of us together share an unbreakable bond. My faith in God, in the source of energy that resides in each and every living thing, has been the core of how I learnt to 'just be'. My perception became skewed for a long time, but I was fooled by the words of others, then I woke up and now I see. It isn't about religion. It's about unity and love. To all! If you open your heart you will see God in every living thing, all around you. All the time! For me God is like the stars, always there, even when you can't see them.

And the very gift God bestowed upon us is freedom. Freedom gives you opportunity. The opportunity to be true to yourself, don't follow anyone down a path...carve your own! Don't let anyone dictate your life...it's yours to live! You want to know the path to your soul? It's the feeling you get when you are listening to music, or walking through the dense trees of a forest, or singing, or playing sports, or climbing mountains, or being with the ones you love, or painting a picture. That feeling that makes you...not feel! You're just there, lightness and freedom envelope you. Time and space disappear, making the experience more than words can convey, more than a feeling. Well that 'none feeling' is it. It's your soul. It's where you should be! Be true to who you are! The best way to make your dreams come true...is to wake up!!

'She's got a ticket, I think she gonna use it, think she goin' to fly away. No one should try and stop her, persuade her with their power she says that her mind is made...'! (25) **Tracey Chapman**

My song comes on the radio, and I smile, as I sit in my new care waiting for my boys, and I knew it was another sign from the universe. I was waiting for Joseph outside his school, then I would meet Francis after he had finished work, and collect Dj from his school. I had told them over breakfast I had a surprise waiting for them when they got home, I hadn't let any of them know what it was. I wanted to see the look on their faces when they saw my surprise.

After collecting Dj we all jumped into the car.

"What's the surprise then mather?" inquired Francis.

"Yeah mummy what is it?" an excited Dj asked.

"I've been excited all day mammy-doo now please tell us!!" Joseph pleaded.

"You are going to have to wait and see!" I said. We drove onwards, the boys quizzing me the entire way. I just smiled to myself, knowing they was about to see the fruition of what I had been working so hard to achieve. Our very own beautiful home! We rounded a corner of a quiet street, Francis turned towards me with a knowing look that said he knew where this was going. We pulled up outside a very elegant five-bedroom home, that stood graciously within its own grounds. The 'For Sale' sign hung over the sandstone wall, covering the top was a vast scattering of overgrown ivy; the word 'sold' was attached to the sign giving them all the clues they needed. The gates to the drive where closed.
I handed Dj a fob and said...
"Do you want to press that?"
"What!!! No way!! Mum...really...really?" Joseph excitedly asked.
Francis just sat there all smiley; proudly and quietly looking over at his mum.
"Did you buy a house mummy...did you?" Dj pressed the fob and the gates opened...

Notes

(1) "I'm in the mood for dancing" – The Nolans
(2) "Be without you" – Mary J Blige
(3) "There must be an Angel" – Eurythmics
(4) "It must be love" – Madness
(5) "Father and Son" – Cat Stevens (Yusuf Islam)
(6) "Snow is falling" – Shakin Stevens
(7) "To Zion" – Lauren Hill
(8) "Beautiful boy" – John Lennon
(9) "The first cut is the deepest" – PP Arnold
(10) "You gotta be" – Des'ree
(11) "Help me make it through the night" – Gladys Knight
(12) "Street Life" – Randy Crawford
(13) "Midnight train to Georgia" – Gladys Knight
(14) "Fairytale of New York" – The Pogues
(15) "Last Christmas" – Wham
(16) "Midnight train to Georgia" – Gladys Knight
(17) "Clown" – Emeli Sande
(18) "Wisdom" – Bob Marley
(19) "Dream the impossible dream" – Man of La Macha
(20) "Father and Son" – Cat Stevens (Yusuf Islam)
(21) "Respectable" – Mel & Kim
(22) "Turn your lights down low" – Bob Marley
(23) "Raindrops keep fallin' on my head" – BJ Thomas
(24) "My Way" – Frank Sinatra
(25) "She's got a ticket" – Tracy Chapman

Printed in Great Britain
by Amazon